Essential
Food & Drink
Spain

by Pepita Aris

Above: *picking grapes in the vineyards of Monovar*

PASSPORT BOOKS
NTC/Contemporary Publishing Group

This edition first published in 2001 by Passport Books, a division of NTC/ Contemporary Publishing Group, Inc., 4255 West Touhy Avenue, Lincolnwood (Chicago), Illinois 60712–1975 U.S.A.

Above: *seasonal produce for sale on market day*
Front cover: *a typical Spanish restaurant; Seville oranges;* Paella *and wine*
Back cover: *a range of the interesting Spanish drink*

The contents of this publication are believed correct at the time of printing. Nevertheless, the publishers cannot accept responsibility for errors or omissions, nor for changes in details given. We are always grateful to readers who let us know of any errors or omissions they come across, and future printings will be updated accordingly.

Published by Passport Books in conjunction with The Automobile Association of Great Britain.

Written by Pepita Aris

Library of Congress Catalog Card Number: 00-136137
ISBN 0-658-01464-1

Colour separation: Chroma Graphics (Overseas) Pte Ltd, Singapore

Printed and bound in Italy by Printer Trento srl

Contents

About this Book

One of the pleasures of travelling is sampling the local food and drink. Whether your tastes are adventurous or conservative, this book will whet your appetite and give you a genuine taste of Spain. The perfect companion to any meal, it may change your ideas about what is on offer – it is not all *tapas* and PAELLA.

Not only will this book help you to appreciate the true flavours of the country, it will enable you to cope with new or unfamiliar situations, taking the worry out of getting what you want.

This book is organised in the following sections:

FOOD OF SPAIN
Spain's regions are colourfully described, with

the emphasis on local foods and specialities and a look at the influences and traditions that you can still detect in them.

A comprehensive A–Z covers both the foods you are likely to see in shops and markets and the dishes on menus, with star ratings to help you make choices. Where items in this list appear elsewhere in the text they are printed in small capitals, thus GAZPACHO.

WINE AND DRINK OF SPAIN
There is information and advice on wines along with an A–Z of other drinks, both alcoholic and non-alcoholic, also star rated.

EATING OUT
The Eating Out section can help you decide where to eat and at what time. There are also tips on catering for babies and children and special diets.

EATING IN
The guide to shopping describes the different types of establishments and what services they offer and what you can buy (including recommended picnic food).

The recipes, using typical Spanish ingredients like peppers and chillies, garlic and sherry, will appeal to cooks of all abilities.

PRACTICAL INFORMATION
A highly visual section containing essential information like coping with a tight budget and planning a self-catering holiday.

A short section highlights the types of food and dishes eaten on high days and holidays and advises on what is seasonally available.

Understanding the menu can sometimes be a problem and the language section gives useful phrases to use in a variety of establishments, as well as a pronunciation guide.

Finally, there is a conversion table to help with shopping and cooking.

Tantalising display of fruit in Barcelona's La Boquería market

Food of
Spain

Above: *sardines are caught off the Cantábrica coast*
Right: *ensaimada, a speciality of Mallorca*

Food of Spain

For almost 1,000 years after its conquest by the Arabs in AD 711, Spain's cultural links were with North Africa. As the Arab Moors were driven out, they were replaced by a number of separate kingdoms. Though the country united in 1474, provinces like the Basque country and Catalunya have continued to assert their individuality. This regionalism is reflected in the cooking.

Another important factor was the discovery of America in 1492. From the new lands came chocolate, as well as tomatoes, peppers, potatoes, maize, sugar cane and numerous varieties of beans. The Spanish adopted them all and invented recipes to make use of them long before they became familiar elsewhere. During the 16th century it was Italian chefs who raised the reputation of the new Spanish restaurants.

The French contribution came when *nouvelle cuisine* inspired the Basques to their own *nueva cocina basca*. The Spanish cooks adopted the aspects of this new style that suited them – the results were better versions of the local dishes that they had always made, produced with a new confidence.

Cooking seafood Paella

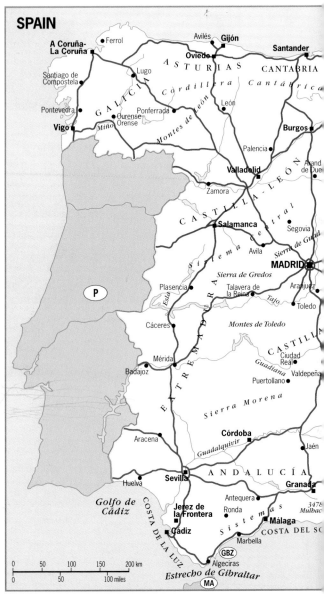

SPAIN

A Coruña-La Coruña
Ferrol
Avilés
Gijón
Santander
Oviedo
ASTURIAS CANTABRIA
Lugo
Cordillera Cantábrica
Santiago de Compostela
León
GALICIA
Pontevedra
Ponferrada
Montes de León
Burgos
Ourense
Orense
Vigo
Miño
Palencia
Aranda de Due
Valladolid
CASTILLA-LEÓN
Zamora
Central
Salamanca
Sistema
Segovia
Ávila
Sierra de Guad
MADRID
Sierra de Gredos
Plasencia
Talavera de la Reina
Aranjuez
Tajo
P
Esla
Toledo
Montes de Toledo
Cáceres
CASTILLA
Mérida
Ciudad Real
Guadiana
Badajoz
Valdepeña
Puertollano
Sierra Morena
EXTREMADURA
Aracena
Córdoba
Jaén
Guadalquivir
Sevilla
ANDALUCÍA
Granada
Huelva
Antequera
3478 Mulhac
Ronda
Golfo de Cádiz
Jerez de la Frontera
Málaga
Sistemas
COSTA DE LA LUZ
Cádiz
Marbella
COSTA DEL SO
GBZ
Algeciras
Estrecho de Gibraltar
MA

| 0 | 50 | 100 | 150 | 200 km |
| 0 | | 50 | | 100 miles |

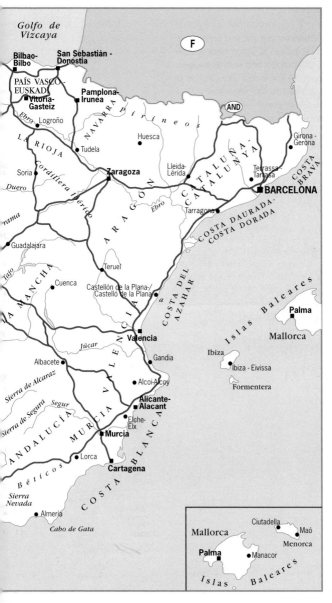

Golfo de Vizcaya

Bilbao-Bilbo

San Sebastián - Donostia

PAÍS VASCO-EUSKADI

Vitoria-Gasteiz

Pamplona-Irunea

F

Logroño

Ebro

LA RIOJA

NAVARRA

Pirineos

AND

Huesca

Tudela

Soria

Cordillera Ibérica

Zaragoza

Lleida-Lérida

CATALUÑA-CATALUNYA

Girona-Gerona

COSTA BRAVA

Tetrassa-Tarrasa

BARCELONA

Duero

rama

Guadalajara

Tajo

LA MANCHA

Cuenca

Teruel

ARAGON

Ebro

Tarragona

COSTA DAURADA-COSTA DORADA

Castellón de la Plana-Castelló de la Plana

COSTA DEL AZAHAR

Islas Baleares

Palma

Mallorca

Júcar

Valencia

VALENCIA

Albacete

Gandia

Ibiza

Ibiza - Eivissa

Sierra de Alcaraz

Alcoi-Alcoy

Formentera

Sierra de Segura

Segur

Alicante-Alacant

ANDALUCÍA

MURCIA

Elche-Elx

Murcia

COSTA BLANCA

Lorca

Cartagena

Béticos

Sierra Nevada

Almería

Cabo de Gata

Mallorca

Ciutadella

Maó

Menorca

Palma

Manacor

Islas Baleares

Regions

Spain is a country of fierce regional pride. Wherever you are, just here in this particular corner of Spain, you will be told, grow the best beans, or asparagus, or peppers in the world. The cooking is well-matched to the ingredients and recipes are regional – or develop their regional variations.

ANDALUCÍA

In Andalucía you will find the essence of all that is Spain – flamenco dancing, bull-fighting and brown *sierras* (mountains) – often topped by the black bull silhouette that splendidly advertises Veterano brandy. It is a huge area of the south, cut off from central Spain by the Sierra Morena.

The Arabs marked the landscape by planting olives and oranges. They created a cuisine based on spices like cumin and saffron, and ingredients such as olive oil and nuts, all ground with mortar and pestle. Their

chilled soups, such as the white garlic and almond AJO BLANCO, made with local muscat grapes, and GAZPACHO (now made with tomato and pepper) are welcome in the summer heat. It is here that *tapas* were invented, to sustain evenings that end in a mere five hours' sleep. One of the best *tapa* is sliced SERRANO, raw ham cured above the winter snow line at places like Trevélez.

The Costa del Sol is celebrated for its fried fish. The fried fish take-away was invented here in the great seaport of Cádiz, and the city is now known for its PESCAÍTO FRITO (mixed fried fish), while each beach-bar on the coast offers squid rings in batter. Málaga is famous for deep-fried little CHANQUETES (gobies, or other tiny fish) and fresh anchovies, with their tails stuck together then fried in the shape of a fan. The area is also known for skate with paprika, grilled swordfish steaks and fish soups, like

An olive plantation near Jaén, in Andalucía

CALDILLO DE PERRO. A fish stew worth searching out is URTA A LA ROTEÑA.

From Jerez de la Frontera, where your sample of Fino is hurled through the air into a glass, come sherry dishes such as kidneys in sherry or stewed bull's tail (RABO DE TORO A LA JEREZANA). In Seville 'duck with orange' was invented (PATO A LA SEVILLANA).

Tomatoes and peppers were first introduced here 400 years ago and appear in many local dishes, like PIPIRRANA (pepper salad) and flamenco eggs, the colourful gypsy mixture of different vegetables with eggs. Another traveller's dish is OLLA GITANA, a stew which can include any vegetable or fruit.

Desserts in the south are eaten in small spoonfuls as they are incredibly sweet, like quince paste and TOCINO DE CIELO, a jelly of syrup and egg yolks.

The best, however, are the little Arab cakes, such as the almond ALFAJORES of Medina Sidonia and the crumbly POLVORONES in Antequera. Try also the YEMAS, which are rich little egg yolk candies, made by nuns.

LEVANTE

Named for 'where the east wind blows', the Levante takes in most of the east coast, from Cartagena northwards. It includes the orange-growing areas of Alicante and Valencia – and a good many sunshine beaches, like Benidorm. This is the land that the legendary medieval hero El Cid won back from the Moors.

But the Arabs introduced rice, and Valencia is the home of the famous PAELLA – originally cooked outdoors – and other rice and fish dishes, including ARROZ A BANDA and EL CALDERO. Rice is also partnered with beans in the black and white dish MOROS Y CRISTIANOS (Moors and Christians).

The market gardens here produce wonderful vegetables, while the big Albufera lake yeilds both ducks and eels. ANGUILA AL ALI-PEBRE is a spicy way of serving the latter.

The most famous fish dish of this area is DORADA A LA SAL, bass baked in salt, but the

Oranges are a familiar sight on the landscape in the south

grey mullet is also good, as is an unusual brown mussel (*dantil de mar*). Other specialities include cured fish, like MOJAMA and GIRABOIX, which is a salted cod stew. The coast is also a centre for pickled capers – delicious with fried fish.

As well as oranges, figs and muscat grapes are plentiful, while Elx-Elche has the world's largest date grove. A milky summer drink to try is HORCHATA, made from tiger nuts, while the whole of Spain buys almond TURRÓN from Jijona at Christmas.

CATALUNYA AND THE BALEARICS

Catalynya (also known as Cataluña or Catalonia) embraces both the Pyrenees (Pirineos) and the Costa Brava. Barcelona restaurants have been famous for over 100 years and the city is now one of Europe's best places to eat.

ZARZUELA and SUQUET, two ebullient fish stews that burst with shellfish, are made here, as is the wonderful crazy mixture

◄ *The village of Serra de l'Albera, Catalonia, surrounded by lush green vineyards*

LANGOSTA CON POLLA (lobster with chicken), while LANGOSTA A LA CATALANA is likely to be lobster with chocolate!

PARRILLADA is a grilled dish which includes fish and shellfish (or fish with meat), often with chilli and nut ROMESCO sauce. Salted cod is so popular here that it is sold ready-soaked, for dishes like XATÓ, the Tarragona salad. Or try the pasta and shellfish mix called FIDEUÀ. Duck with figs, or gosling with pears, are characteristic poultry and fruit combinations, while duck with olive and rabbit with snails are other celebrated pairings. Vich is known for charcuterie, and excellent black and white BUTIFARRA sausages are made here.

Grills are a speciality including COSTELLADA, lamb chops with local sausage, eaten with pungent ALIOLI (garlic sauce). Indeed, barbecues produce some of the best food, like ESCALIVADA (baked whole vegetables), barbecued spring onions eaten at the feast called *calçotada*, and grilled snails, eaten at the CARGOLADA feast. In winter, warming vegetable stews such as ESCUDELLA DE PAGÉS are a welcome feast, and wild mushrooms, particularly ROVELLÓN, are a passion.

Well-prepared spinach, ESPINACAS A LA CATALANA, is eaten with the flat bread called *coca*. And you will find that in Catalunya all meals start with a tomato bread called PA AMB TOMÀQUET.

The English occupied Menorca in the Balearic Isles (Islas Baleares) in the 18th century – and left gin and gravy (*grevi*) behind as proof! The French found MAHONESA (mayonnaise) there in the 1770s, and took the recipe home. But the Balearics are best known for very solid, heavy dishes made with lots of bread, like SOPA MALLORQUINA, and vegetable stews like TUMBET. Stuffed squid, fried poultry in sauce (ESCALDUMS), and SOBRASADA (a soft red sausage) are other local dishes. The pizza-like COCAS MALLORQUINAS are traditionally baked in outdoor ovens, and pies, large and small, are island favourites. There is a local cheese, too – MAHÓN.

Catalunya gave the world a favourite dessert, *crème brûlée* (CREMA CATALANA), but try also the almond cream (MENJAR BLANCO), and simple curds with honey (MEL I MATÓ). PANELLETS and ROSCOS in Barcelona and BUNYOLS on the coast are among the little cakes to look out for.

NEW CASTILE AND LA MANCHA

High on Spain's central plateau, this is Don Quixote and windmill country, centred on the nation's capital. The temperatures here are extreme – bitter winter cold and parching summer heat.

Madrid is home to all styles of cooking, with many good authentic regional restaurants. It also has a robust nightlife.

Its most famous meat dishes are COCIDO MADRILEÑO, where several meats are simmered together for hours, and a beloved nursery dish of stewed tripe (CALLOS) found in all the tapas bars. You will also find good roast meat, baked bream (BESUGO AL HORNO) and a local salted cod dish, SOLDADITOS DE PAVÍA To the south, near the exquisite former

Windmills of La Mancha are a prominent feature of the region

royal summer palace at Aranjuez, strawberries and asparagus grow.

Castile (Castilla) is the country's bread basket, growing excellent wheat, pure and very white; from it a distinctive round bread is made – and also wheat soup. The bread is the ideal accompaniment for the local tomato stew (PISTO MANCHEGO). Beans and lentils are local crops, while Zamora is chickpea country. The plains also grow Spain's 'yellow gold' – saffron, the world's most expensive spice. And it is said that TORTILLA, the national egg dish, has its origins in Castile, invented by a peasant for a hungry king.

Castile is the partridge capital of Spain. The bird is used for *perdiz estofada* (braised partridge) and jellied ESCABECHE, besides mixed game pâtés like GAZPACHO MANCHEGO and MORTERUELO.

The plains are famous for sheep, and for the country's most distinguished cheese, Manchego. Try it breadcrumbed and fried as QUESO FRITO, Madrid *fiestas* are well known for their sweet pastries, like the cream-filled BUÑUELOS and the sugared bread TORRIJA, made for children. Toledo, the old capital, is famous for MAZAPÁN, made into little *figuras* for Christmas. The wine-soaked cakes, BIZCOCHOS BORRACHOS, can be eaten in any season.

OLD CASTILE AND RIOJA

Cut off from Madrid to the south by the Guardarrama mountains (Sierra de Guadarrama), Old Castile runs north to the Cordillera Cantábrica. Three great medieval cities are sited here – Avila, Salamanca and Segovia.

This is the centre of the *zona de asados*, for here the best roasts are prepared in the old beehive Arab ovens, called *hornos de asar*, characteristic of Segovia, Valladolid and Burgos. The secret is that the meat is not cooked quickly, as you might expect for young animals, but roasted gently and slowly for succulence. At Avila and Segovia, COCHINILLO (suckling pig) is an institution,

Peppers from La Rioja, a mainstay of Spanish cooking

though LECHAZO (milk-fed lamb) is sometimes rated even higher. The Rioja also grows wonderful peppers; indeed dishes with 'a la riojana' in their name are likely to include them, for example PATATAS A LA RIOJANA. Lots of beans are grown and eaten dried, as well as green, and fresh beans (POCHAS) are eaten with quail or sausage. Baked aubergines and white asparagus, sold in cans throughout Spain, are other specialities, Castilian garlic soup is well known, especially at Avila. The monastery there also makes the sugary yellow cakes called YEMAS.

ARAGÓN AND NAVARRA

Aragón and Navarra embrace the northern end of the Pyrenees and their foothills, a country dotted with monasteries, for pilgrims poured through Roncesvalles and other valleys on the pilgrim route to Santiago de Compostela, one of Europe's holiest Catholic shrines. With them they brought French-style dishes like MENESTRA DE VERDURAS (a vegetable stew). One simple traveller's dish is salted cod in BACALAO AL AJOARRIERO.

Mountains mean good lamb, grilled as chops, roasted young as TENASCO, or stewed as COCHIFRITO. Here 'mountain asparagus' means lambs' tails, lopped in spring! Real asparagus grows at Tudela and is used in Tortillas. The foothills slope down to the banks of the warm Ebro river, where red peppers are grown, in particular the slim and very spicy PIMIENTOS DEL PIQUILLO. At Lodosa these peppers are protected by an *appellation contrôlée*, and eaten stuffed with meat or salted cod. The region is even better known for red pepper stews called *chilindrones*.

Fast streams in the mountains breed trout, and *truchas a la Navarra* are fried in ham fat and served stuffed or wrapped in ham. The opening of the hunting season is celebrated with POCHAS CON CODORNICES, the first quails, eaten with fresh kidney beans. Partridges are often deliciously served with chocolate sauce. Rabbit is stewed with garlic, wine and rosemary, while fried sausages with eggs are popular, too.

The black Aragón MORCILLA sausage includes both rice and pine nuts, while the CHORIZO of Pamplona-Irunea is simply the best *tapa* sausage.

Hidden in the Pyrenees, the Val d'Arran was once cut off from the rest of Spain for six months of the year by bad weather until Franco built a tunnel to it. Now skiing has made the area fashionable, and good chefs

Garlic: a love of this pungent bulb is an advantage in Spain

have rushed to open *bordas*, 'barn restaurants', where the food is earthy but invariably good. Local specialities include pigeon with raisins (PICHÓN CON PASAS PIÑONES). Aragón has its own cheese in RONCAL. It is also known for junket (CUAJADA), sold in brown pots resembling flower pots and eaten with honey. The foothills bear orchards of apple, cherry and peach, and peaches in red wine are a delicious local delicacy.

BASQUE COUNTRY AND CANTABRICAN COAST

In their tiny corner of Spain, snuggled next to the Bay of Biscay (Golfo de Vizcaya) and the mountains that lead to France, the Basques are self-styled 'gourmets', with a restaurant for every thousand inhabitants! Here men-only associations, called *cofradías*, cook and eat gourmet meals – the women wash up! Anywhere in Spain, a Basque name on a restaurant (an unpronounceable title with TX in it) means it is likely to be first-rate.

The Basque have traditionally looked outward, beyond their own territory, for influence and inspiration. Firstly there is a French Basque region, too – and dishes like the soft, un-Spanish omelette PIPERRADA prove it. Then Basques are the rovers, the Atlantic fishermen bringing home great catches of cod. Their shipboard stews such as MARMITAKO, and other dishes made with Bonito tuna are well known. Among dozens of salted cod recipes, BACALAO A LA VIZCAÍNA is the most famous.

The area is also celebrated for the most delicate fish dishes, including MERLUZA EN SALSA VERDE (hake in a green parsley and pea sauce), exquisite fried sole, and BACALAO AL PIL-PIL, requiring an especially light chef's touch. The name *donastia* (Basque for San Sebastián), is given to many local dishes, so expect to be a little confused! Other fishy luxuries are TXANGURRO (stuffed crab) and CHIPIRONES EN SU TINTA, best here when squid are line-caught, not in nets where they lose the ink that makes the black sauce of the dish.

The fishing port of Castro Urdiales, on the north coast of Spain

Eating ANGULAS (elvers) in winter started in the Basque eating clubs, and the fashion spread. Another rarity is KOKOTXAS, pieces of hake cut from the throat, best made into fritters.

The Cantabrican coast, where many Spanish families take their holidays, is known for its small fish restaurants. Dishes include clams or baby sardines in sauces, and fresh local trout and salmon. RABA is an unusual squid dish with the squid first coated in breadcrumbs, then fried.

The green Basque countryside grows fresh peas, green beans and artichokes in season, made into casseroles like MENESTRA. It is also known for broad beans, eaten fresh. Dried beans (such as kidney beans) are made into soups like *baba-txikis* or stewed with sausage, like the bean stew of Tolosa. Guernica is famous for *choricero* peppers, used to make local sausages and roast peppers with chops. The Basques make a good leek and potato soup with salted cod (PURRUSALDA), and they are also keen mushroom-hunters.

Local meat is good, with plentiful roasts, enormous steaks and good lamb and game dishes, like CODORNICES EN HOJAS (quails in vine leaves). The Cantabrican coast is known for chicken with rice (CAMPURRIANO). This is also dairy country, however, and the local Basque cheese is smokey IDIAZÁBAL, while a mild blue PASIEGO is made at Pas. Desserts to tempt include custard horns (CAÑUTILLOS) and INTXAURSALSA, an unusual walnut cream.

GALICIA AND ASTURIAS

The extreme west is Spain's Celtic fringe – a misty, green, apple-growing country. The landscape is studded with little *horreos*, sheds built on stilts for storing maize and cheeses. In the far west, the vines are grown up on pergolas, unusual for Spain. In the western bays huge, tender orange mussels grow beneath structures that resemble Chinese junks, and indeed the whole area is famous for its seafood. Dishes to try include LANGOSTA, the excellent lobster, while Santiago de Compostela has its own lobsters (*santiaguiños*) – and of course the pilgrims' scallop dish, VIEIRAS DE SANTIAGO. A strange and costly shellfish is the tubular black barnacle, PERCEDES. At festival time big octopuses are displayed on all the bars, to be served as spicy PULPO AL FERIA. rape (monkfish, called *pixin* here) is coooked in cider. Varieties of fish are placed in layers to make a delicious CALDERETA, while small cuttlefish and sardines are made into pies. Freshwater fish include salmon.

This is tripe and sausage country, home of the black MORCILLA of León, which goes into Austurias' famous bean dish, FABADA. Lentils and chestnuts are also much used. Galicia's best known stew is LACÓN CON GRELOS, a ham knuckle cooked with young turnip tops.

Butter and lard are much used in cooking,

Sweetcorn put out to dry

and a number of meats are cooked in milk. Duck with turnips is claimed as a Galician recipe, and chicken tastes excellent when roasted in pork fat or cooked with beans or rice. There are also many pigeon and partridge dishes. In the wilderness of Asturias, game such as chamoix and caper-cailli is hunted. Local cuisine is simple fare – chestnut soup and CACHELADA, a stew with fine potatoes and CHORIZO, are good examples. Huge heads of cabbage, some a metre (3 feet) high, will catch your eye as you drive through Galicia and these go into broths like CALDO GALLEGO. Many lettuces are grown in this part of Spain, while locals claim watercress was first eaten here. The tiny green peppers from Padrón are sold all over Spain usually to be deep-fried whole.

EMPANADAS are giant pies made with peppers and tomatoes, plus fish or pork, and further inland they may be topped with bread dough, rather than pastry. Rye bread is a local speciality, while cornmeal is used for bread (BORONA) sometimes stuffed with meat (*prenada*).

Spain's most famous creamy blue cheese, CABRALES, comes from Asturias, and distinctive fresh REQUESONES (cottage cheeses) are made. Favourite cheeses include Galician smoked SAN SIMÓN, which looks like an amber pear, and the soft, breast-shaped TETILLA.

Asturias is known for the best milk in Spain and not surprisingly you can enjoy many milk puddings: rice travelled north as ARROZ CON LECHE. Look out too for the varities of sweet pancake, like the Galician liqueur-flavoured FILLOAS. About 250 varieties of apples are grown locally, together with plums and pears. Desserts include apple tarts, pears in red wine with cinnamon (invented here), and superb sugary MARRÓN GLACÉS.

EXTREMADURA

The name means 'extreme and hard' and the west of the region, bordering Portugal, has some of the most beautiful mountain scenery in this mountainous country. Chestnuts, cork oaks and the evergreen holm oak, whose acorns feed the black pigs, grow in abundance.

The most famous ham in Spain is produced at Jabugo, where the snows of the *sierras* give it its popular name, SERRANO – 'mountain' ham. The best hams are those from the wild *pata negra* pig. Superb hams are also made at Montánchez. As you might expect, there are also excellent CHORIZOS and MORCILLAS. In a restaurant an *entremes de carne*, a sliced selection, is one way to try the local cured meat. Sausages also go into the local TORTILLA, while PRINGADAS are bread strips fried in bacon fat. Garlicky croûtons, called MIGAS, are made to eat with savoury dishes, and also served as a sweet with a chocolate sauce!

Local delicacies include frogs, small eels, partridges and turkeys, while the monastery at Alcántara is famous for its luxury pheasant dish (FAISÁN AL MODO DE ALCÁNTARA). Mountain lamb is the meat in the stew, COCHIFRITO; use is also made of tongues, liver, and there is a local kidney dish, RIÑONADA. Jellied ESCABECHE and freshwater tench are also relished.

Farm workers taking in the crop around the upper Extremadura town of Trujillo

A–Z of Spanish Food

A

Abadejo
Pollack. A less flavourful fish than hake (MERLUZA) but cooked the same.

Abichón
Silverside or sand smelt. A good fish when tiny and deep-fried like whitebait.

Acedias fritas ✪✪
Fried baby soles. A popular *tapa* in the southwest.

Aceite de girasol
Sunflower oil.

Aceite de oliva
Olive oil. Usually 'pure' (which is a mixture of virgin and refined oil) and labelled with its acidity – 0.8° is perfect.

Aceitunas
Olives. *Aceitunas aliñadas* are marinated olives, that is, cocktail olives.

Aceitunas rellenas con anchoas ✪✪
Green olives with anchovy stuffing. Newest and nicest of the cocktail olives.

Acelga
Swiss chard or spinach beet. A vegetable with gleaming white stems and bitter dark leaves, that is much loved in the south. You will find it *fritas* and *guisadas* (fried and stewed); in MENESTRA, a general vegetable stew; in rice and bean soup and as a TORTA, which may have a little sugar in it as well.

Acelgas con pasas y pinoñes ✪✪
Chard fried with plump raisins and crisp pine nuts, sometimes called *a la malagueña*. A similar dish, *a la catalana*, includes anchovies.

Achicoria
Chicory.

Aderezada
With dressing. Many canned, cooked vegetables are sold like this.

Aderezo de mesa
Condiments.

Adobo
Marinated before cooking. *Lomo adobado* is marinated pork loin for roasting or frying.

Agua de azahar
Orange flowered water. For flavouring desserts.

Aguacate
Avocado. *Con gambas* means it is stuffed with prawns.

Aguja
Gar or needlefish. A couple of feet (60cm) long and with a nose like a knitting needle. The backbone is green, but do not let this bother you. Good poached.

Agujas, en
On skewers.

Ahumado
Smoked. You can guess *salmón ahumado*.

Ajada, allada ✪
Garlic, paprika and oil beaten to make a sauce. Used to dress hot fish and vegetables.

Ajedrea
Savory (the herb).

Ajetes ✪✪
A springtime speciality of young garlic shoots, pulled from the centre of the bulb. Wonderful with scrambled eggs, they are also pickled as *brotes de ajo*.

Ajiaceite, al
In garlic oil. The simplest of Spanish sauces used, for example, with snails.

Ajilla, en
In a garlic sauce, usually a pan sauce. Often thickened after frying with garlic puréed with bread.

Ajo a
Garlic.

Ajo, al
The dish has whole garlic cloves in it. Do not be too frightened of these; garlic becomes quite mild after long cooking. It is raw garlic that makes the smell!

Ajo arriero
'In the mule-drivers' style', that is, dressed with garlic, paprika and parsley. These chaps were the forerunners of truckers, moving goods across the country. The places they stayed in *en route* were too poor for anything fancy, and these dishes are simple, made with eggs, or vegetables like cauliflower, or salted cod.

Pickled red and green olives mixed with red chilli peppers

Ajo blanco con uvas de Málaga ✪✪✪
A most delicious chilled almond cream soup (white GAZPACHO) flavoured with garlic and finished with muscat grapes.

Ajo colorado ✪✪
Creamy salted cod pounded with bread and garlic and coloured red with paprika. It is a red version of the French *brandade*, and Lent food.

Ajo de la mano, el
Literally 'garlic in the hand', this is potatoes cooked with chillies, then dressed with pounded garlic, cumin, oil and vinegar.

Ajoaceite
Castilian for ALIOLI, usually a smooth dense garlic sauce, with eggs yolks and even mashed potato or breadcrumbs.

Ajonjolí
Sesame seeds. Popular in little festival cakes.

Ajopollo, en
'In the sort of garlic sauce chicken is served in', with almonds; see PEPITORIA.

Alajú ✪✪
A rich, flat medieval cake. Dense, very dark and made with honey and whole toasted almonds, like Italian *panforte*.

Albacora
The long-finned tuna with white flesh. It is less dense than ATÚN, and considered the best tuna.

Albahaca
Basil.

Albardado
Barded (wrapped in fat or fat meat, eg ham), or battered or crumb-coated.

Albaricoque
Apricot. Dried fruit are called OREJONES.

Albóndigas en salsa ✪✪
Meatballs in sauce, usually tomato. A popular *tapa*, they are often made of veal and pork. The same word is often used for fish cakes.

Albufera, salsa ✪✪
A cream and red pepper sauce, sometimes with ground almonds in it. Good with fish.

Alcachofas
The big flower buds of globe artichokes. In the middle of each one is a bristly choke (which has to be removed) above the edible soft base. Prepared bases are often served as salads. *Aliñadas* means 'marinated' and *con mayonesa* is with mayonnaise. They are also included in many salads and hot rice mixtures.

Alcachofas al vinagreta ✪
Artichokes served boiled and warm, or cold, with vinaigrette. To eat, the leaves are pulled off, each base dipped into the sauce, then just the soft flesh pulled off with the teeth.

Alcachofas rellenas ✪✪
Artichokes stuffed in the middle, often *con atún* (tuna).

Alcachofas salteadas con jamón ✪✪
Sautéed artichoke bases with ham. The bases are also braised in Montilla, or served with potatoes, in a saffron broth (see recipe page 106).

Alcaparras
Capers. These grow wild and the pickled flower buds are particularly good with fried fish.

Alcaravea
Caraway seeds.

Alfajores ✪✪✪
An individually-wrapped Christmas almond and honey candy, invented by the Arabs. The ones made in Medina Sidonia are sensational.

Aliño
A simple vinaigrette, or an oil and salt dressing. *Aliñado* means marinated, or dressed, vegetables or fish.

Alioli (all-i-oli) ✪✪✪
This is one of the greatest Spanish sauces, to be tried at least once in a lifetime. Take your vote that either everybody in your party eats it or nobody, because it does make the breath smell quite powerfully, as puréed raw garlic is the main ingredient. This is whisked to an emulsion with oil and sometimes egg yolks too. One of the best sauces for prawns barbecued in the shell and grilled fish or chops, it is also stirred into fish soups. In Catalunya, *aliolis* of puréed fruit and garlic are served with roast lamb.

Almadrote
A sauce of mashed garlic and hard cheese, usually cooked with aubergine.

Almejas ✪✪
Clams. Raw or cooked in wine or spicy tomato sauce, clams are popular seaside fare, though fiddly to eat. In *almejas con arroz*, clams and onions flavour rice.

Almejas a la marinera ✪✪✪
Clams fisherman's style, with white wine, a little oil and parsley.

Almendras, tostadas
Toasted almonds. They are popular with drinks. Everything from soup (*sopa*) to trout (*trucha*) can be made *almendrada*, made from or cooked with almonds. See PEPITORIA for almond sauce with chicken. *Almendras garrapiñadas* are almonds in toasted sugar.

Almíbar, en
In syrup. The Arabs invented syrup, and probably peaches in syrup too.

Alpargatas
The name means *espadrilles* and these 'shoe-shapes' can be sweet biscuits in the north. They can also be meat patties, coated in whisked egg before frying, which gives them the appearance of rope-soled shoes.

Alubias
Dried kidney beans of lots of different

Almonds, found in many dishes

colours. Tolosa is famous for black beans (*alubias negras*). Beans *a la vizcaína* are typical: stewed with a little TOCINO (pork fat), onion, garlic and parsley.

Amanida
The Catalan word for salad. Probably an arranged salad including fish and meat, if it is *a la catalana*.

Amargo
Bitter.

Amargos, amarguillos ✪
Little, dry Arab marzipan cakes.

Amarilla, en ✪✪
A yellow sauce, made from onions and saffron, thickened with egg yolks.

Ametlles ✪✪
Catalan for almonds; also delicious toasted almonds, coated in praline or chocolate.

Ancardos
Cashew nuts.

Anchoas
Canned anchovies. *En aceite* (in oil).

Andaluz, salsa ✪
Andalucían sauce. Usually includes garlic, tomatoes, peppers and pumpkin. *A la andaluza* is with red peppers and tomato.

Añejo
Aged (of cheese etc).

THE DIVERSITY OF RICE

Rice is used to make many simple dishes in Spain, like ENSALADA (rice salad) and is combined with all sorts of different ingredients, such as BUTIFARRA sausage, chicken giblets, fried bananas, fish, pig's cheek and trotters, and much more.

In the north, rice dishes are called ARROZ, when they would be called PAELLA in Valencia.

✪✪ Arrós amb crosta (Catalan)/arroz con costra (Castilian) A famous PAELLA, with meatballs, pieces of poultry and pork, cooked in the oven. The egg crust is broken when the dish is served.

✪✪✪ Arroz negre Black rice. It is a speciality of the Costa Brava. Cuttlefish colour the rice with their ink.

✪✪✪ Arroza a banda A famous two-course Valencian fish and rice dish. The rice, flavoured with saffron and fish stock, is served first. The fish, which were cooked in the stock, then follow, often with ALIOLI.

✪✪ Arroz con leche A cold rice pudding, flavoured with lemon and cinnamon. Popular in the northwest. *Requemado* has a grilled sugar top.

Angelote
Angelfish, and a small shark, with a tail like RAPE, but less good to eat.

Anguila
Freshwater eel. *Angula* is elver – baby eel. These look like silver spaghetti and are an expensive luxury in winter.

Anguila al ali-pebre ✪✪
Valencian speciality of eels in an oil and paprika sauce.

Angulas a la bilbaína or en cazuela ✪✪✪
A Basque speciality of baby eels tossed in chilli oil and served from an earthenware casserole with wooden forks.

Anís
Aniseed. One of the great flavours of Spain, much used for biscuits by adding one of the many anís-flavoured liquors.

Anona
Custard apple.

Apio
Celery; *apio ensalada*, celery salad.

Araña
Weever fish. For soup.

Arándano
Bilberry.

Arencas
Salted and pressed sardines.

Arenque
Herrings, usually fried simply.

Arete
Red gurnard. A fish with firm white flesh, of good flavour and not-to-difficult bones. As it is slightly dry, it is best cooked in sauce.

Arrope ✪
A grape juice or honey syrup. Used for sweetening wine and for simmering dried fruit.

Arrós/arroz ✪
Rice (see box above)

Asado
From the oven, so roasted. *Asadillo* is roast, skinned peppers reheated in little dishes with garlic.

Atascaburras ✪✪
On the east coast, this is a purée of salted cod with potato and pine nuts, similar to the French *brandade*. The name is also given to a heavily garlicked rabbit stew – see CONEJO.

Atún ✪✪
Blue-fin tuna. It is a treat fish, grilled in big (bloody) steaks or baked. It may be cooked, marinated and served cold (*escabeche*), or made into small hot pies (*empanadillas*). See also ALBACORA, called *atún blanco*.

Avellana
Hazelnuts. Popular in sauces and pâtisserie.

Avena
Oats.

Azafrán
Saffron. This Arab spice is much included in rice and stews in the north as well as the south. It is always expensive, but beware of imitations if you are buying it to cook!

Azahar
Orange blossom.

Azúcar
Sugar. *Azúcar moreno* is brown sugar – *azucarillos* is candy floss.

B

Bacalao ⊙⊙⊙
Cod. Not a Mediterranean fish, though it may be fresh on the Atlantic coast. It is hugely popular salted and dried, and much eaten in Lent. It does not taste salty after soaking. Leave it 24 hours in a bowl of cold water, under a dribbling tap. It soon makes the water smelly, so the water must be changed regularly. Then remove all skin and bones and cook as fresh. In Catalunya cod is called *bacallá* and is cooked *en samfaina* (in tomato sauce). It is good fried in fingers (*soldaditos*), makes tasty BUÑUELOS (deep-fried potato puffs), and wonderful salads like ESQUEIXADA.

Bacalao a la vizcaína ⊙⊙⊙
The most famous hot dish made with cod. The sauce includes the piquant peppers of the region and sweet ÑORA chillies. Well-

made, it is wonderful, but it can be pretty grim: fish, pools of oil and sparse, too-spicy pepper. Outside the Basque country, the sauce often includes tomatoes too. *Bacalao al la riojana* is very similar, with peppers and paprika.

Bacalao al ajo arriero
Salted cod mashed with garlic and parsley. It is always a pale dish, but can contain scrambled egg.

Bacalao pil-pil ⊙
A Basque dish of hot salted cod. It is gently rocked in the casserole until the gelatine from the fish makes an emulsion, and so a very light white sauce, just from cooking oil and garlic.

Bajoques farcides ⊙⊙
Red peppers stuffed with rice and meat or BACALAO.

Bandarillo
A cocktail stick with bits of cheese or ham; named after the barbed stick used in the bullfight.

Barbacoa, de
Barbecued.

Tuna caught off the coast of Castro Urdiales, accompanied by green chillies

Barquillo
A thin rolled wafer, made on a mould.

Bartolillos ✪✪
Triangles filled with custard, then deep-fried
– a speciality of Madrid.

Batata
Sweet (white) potato.

Becadas ✪✪
Woodcock. They are
roasted or pot-
roasted and may be
stuffed with their
own gizzards, or these may
be pounded for the sauce.

Beicón, bacon
Leanish pink breakfast bacon.

Berberechos
Cockles. Less sweet than clams, they are
made into sauces or served in soup or rice.

Berenjenas
Aubergines. Introduced by the Arabs. *Al
horno* is baked, *fritas* is fried and they are
also moulded (*molde*).

Berenjenas a la catalana ✪
Fried aubergines cooked in tomato sauce.

Berenjenas rellenas ✪✪
Stuffed aubergines with minced beef as well
as garlic, breadcrumbs and chopped egg,
sometimes fish.

*Sardines toasting over hot coals – the smell is
mouth-watering*

Berros
Watercress.

Berza
Green cabbage. Often included in soups or
MENESTRA. *Bertón* is a stuffed cabbage.

Berza andaluza ✪
A mixture of chick-peas or dried beans with
cabbage, ACELGA or green beans, flavoured
with salt pork or other bits of the pig.

Besugo ✪✪✪
Red bream, with a black spot on the
shoulder. A favourite fish in Spain, it is
good grilled or baked with lemon and oil (*a la
madileña*) or in white wine (*al vino blanco*).

Besugo a la donastiarra ✪✪✪
Red bream grilled over a charcoal fire.

Besugo asado con piriñaca ✪✪✪
Baked bream with chopped red peppers.

Bien me sabe
Means 'I know it does me good', given as an
excuse to eat something delicious. There is
a fish dish and also a very rich Andalucian
dessert of ground almonds and cinnamon
with this name.

Biftek, bistek
Beef steak. Ask for it *poco hecho* for rare,
regular or *muy hecho*.

Biftek salteado al jerez ✪✪
Fried steak with a little sherry used to make
a sauce with the cooking juices.

Bizcocho
Sponge cake. The word covers all types,

even sponge finger biscuits. It may be *de almendras* (with almonds) or *a la crema* (with cream).

Bizcochos borrachos ✪✪
'Drunken' cakes soaked in wine or syrup, then sugared.

Bocadillo ✪
A sandwich of a crusty roll, sprinkled inside with olive oil and often filled with ham and cheese.

Bocadillos de monja ✪
This 'nun's mouthful', is a small cake made of almonds, sugar and eggs.

Bocadito
A 'mouthful' – often found on biscuit packets.

Bogovante
The true lobster.

Bola ✪
Béchamel-based croquette, served deep-fried.

Boleto
Cep mushrooms.

Bolets amb peril ✪✪
A simple dish of ceps and ham.

Bollo
A common word for a bread roll, also a sweet bun; (see also SUIZOS). *Bollos de panizo* is a cornmeal scone, eaten with vegetables. *Bollo preñado* – 'pregnant roll' – has meats cooked inside.

Bomba
Meatball, or potato shape, served with chilli sauce.

Bombón
A chocolate.

Boniato
The orange-fleshed sweet potato: America's 'yam'. It is made into sweet puddings with cinnamon; cooked then dipped into syrup; and puréed.

Bonito ✪✪✪
Means 'pretty', and this light, white fleshed tuna, with a dark striped back, is highly prized. It is good grilled or baked, and makes MARMITAKO.

Boquerones ✪
Fresh anchovies. They taste quite different from canned ones (ANCHOAS). The best ones come from L' Escala. They are marinated and served pickled as an *ensalada* or *en vinagreta*.

Boquerones a la malagueña ✪✪
Fresh anchovies stuck together at the tail to form a fan, then floured and fried.

Borona
Cornmeal bread.

Borra, la, borreta ✪✪
A salted cod and potato soup with spinach, flavoured with sweet chilli.

Borracho
Grey gurnard (fish), with firm but dry white flesh. Best baked.

Borrachos, borrachuelos ✪✪
These 'drunkards' are doughnuts or cakes soaked in wine or syrup.

Botifarra amb mongetes ✪✪
Catalan BUTIFARRA sausage stewed with dried white beans.

Bou estofat, buey estofado ✪✪
Catalan beef stew, with sweet RANCIO wine, BUTIFARRA, potatoes and possibly wild mushrooms.

Bover
A large edible snail; see CARACOLES.

Brasa, a la ✪✪
Grilled on a grid over the embers (*brasas*). Meat *a la brasa de sarmiento* is cooked over vine prunings. The best!

Brasear
To braise.

Brazo de gitano ✪✪
'Gypsy's arm'. A well-known cake, like a Swiss roll, but brown, longer and thinner. It is rolled up with cream or chocolate custard. There is also a version with potato.

Breca
Small bream. Good grilled or baked; see DENTÓN.

Brécol, bróculi
Broccoli. *Broquil* in Catalunya, where it is very popular.

Brevas ✪
Small yeast doughnuts, deep-fried with a custard filling. *Breva* is also the black early-ripening fig.

Brocheta
A skewer or spit.

Brotes
Sprouts, bean sprouts or, in the Basque country, the spring side shoots of cabbage.

Buey
Ox, so stewing beef.

Buey
The big-clawed crab.

Bullit
The Mallorcan version of COCIDO.

Buñuelos ✪✪
Fried puffs, often served as *tapas*. The lightest ones are made of choux pastry, with additions – like *buñuelos de queso* (cheese puffs). *Buñuelos de bacalao* are often based on mashed potato – a good way to try out salted cod. Others are coated, crisp fried morsels; like *sesos*, made with brains, which are very creamy inside, or *apio*, from celery. Sweet fritters are made from apricot (*albaricoque*) and puffs are soaked in syrup (*al aguamiel*).

Buñuelos de viento ✪✪
Choux puffs 'as light as the wind' says the name. San Isidro is celebrated in Madrid with cream-filled ones.

Bunyettes
Yeast doughnuts.

Bunyols ✪✪
Warm, sugared, deep-fried doughnuts. Popular on the Costa Brava, sometimes cream-filled.

Burgos, queso de ✪✪
A fresh ewes milk cheese, a bit like a drum-shaped mozzarella.

Búsano
Whelk.

Butifarra ✪✪✪
A big banger, the white sausage made from pork or veal, of Catalunya. It is frequently cooked with beans (*con habas*). There are also black *butifarrones*.

C

Caballa
Common mackerel. An oily fish, it is best baked (*al horno*) – good *a la gaditana* – or stewed with potatoes. See also ESTORNINO.

Cabello de ángel
'Angel's hair' comes from a squash (CIDRA), with very stringy flesh. It is stewed or made into a popular jam, which is much used in shop pastries.

Choose from tempting displays of local produce

Cabeza de ternera
A 'head-cheese' (ie a seasoned loaf) of jellied veal. *Cabeza de cerdo* is brawn.

Cabra ✪✪
Goat. Both *cabrito asado* (young goat) and *caldereta de cabra* (stewed kid) are good.

Cabracho
The ugly, spiny, copper-red scorpion fish. A great soup-stew ingredient.

Cabrales ✪✪✪
A creamy blue cheese. A cheese to challenge Roquefort, and, like it, stored in limestone caves, where it acquires its blue veining. It is generally made of cows' milk and shaped like a small drum without pressing. It is finally wrapped in maple leaves.

Cabrillo
Comber (fish). Used for soup, although the tail is worth eating.

Cacahuetes
Peanuts.

Cachelada ✪✪
A Galician stew using the new potatoes called *cachelos* with CHORIZO.

Cailón ✪
Porbeagle shark. Good to eat, especially the barbecued steaks.

Calabacines
Courgettes. They are baked (*al horno*), stuffed (*rellenos*) and made into fritters (*fritos*).

Calabaza guisada
Stewed pumpkin, often included in vegetable sauces in the south. *Calabazote* is a pumpkin, potato and bean stew.

Calamares ✪✪
Squid. Batter-fried squid rings (*a la romana*), are a common *tapa*. Small ones are cooked in their own ink, *en su tinta*, in the north – see CHIPIRONES. In the south, small *calamaritos* are often served in a tomato, pepper, paprika and fish sauce.

Calamares rellenos ✪✪
Stuffed squid. The stuffing may be pork and almonds (*a la catalana*), or grated cheese with pine nuts, breadcrumbs and parsley (*a la levantina*); in Mallorca raisins are added.

Calçots ✪✪✪
A Catalan word for spring onions as thick as a finger, which are a speciality of Valls in

29

Tarragona. At la *calçotada*, a spring feast, they are eaten direct from the barbecue with ROMESCO sauce.

Caldereta de cordero ✪✪✪
Stewed lamb. This is particularly good when thickened by the lamb's liver. In Extremadura it also includes red peppers, MIGAS and the local sausage as well; in Seville, a good slug of sherry. There are also quail (*codornices*) and rabbit (*conejo*) versions.

Caldereta de pescados ✪✪✪
On the north coast this is layered fish casserole, often with potatoes, and there are versions with shellfish and even lobster (*langosta*). These may be served liquid first, as soup, then the fish.

Caldero
A cooking pot or small cauldron. *Caldereta*, *caldeirada* are the stews that come out of it. *El caldero* on the south coast is a soupy rice and fish dish.

Caldillo de perro ✪✪
Little 'dog soup'. It is made of fresh small hake, flavoured with bitter orange juice and is a speciality of Puerto de Santa María on Cádiz harbour.

Caldo gallego ✪✪
A hearty Galician soup, containing white beans, turnip tops and a ham bone.

Caliente
Hot.

Callos
Stewed tripe. Popular in *tapas* bars across Spain.

Callos a la catalana ✪✪
Stewed tripe dish which may include pine nuts and rich RANCIO wine.

Callos a la madrileña ✪✪
Typical stewed tripe dish. Highly spiced with ham and CHORIZO. Chick-peas are often included, as they are in Galicia and Andalucía.

Camarones ✪✪
Tiny shrimp, white in Cádiz.

Camerano, queso de ✪
A soft, fresh goats' milk cheese from Rioja.

Campurriano
'From the country' (*campo*). *Pollo campurriano* in Santander is a rice dish with

chicken, bacon, peppers, shallots and wine.

Caña de dulce
Sugar cane; also a puff pastry finger with custard filling.

Caña de vaca
Marrow bone.

Cañadilla, cañailla
Sea snail, like a whelk with knobs on. Eaten cold as a starter. This is the *murex* from which the Roman Imperial purple dye came. It will not stain your mouth though, as the dye only develops when exposed to the sun.

Canela, con
With cinnamon. This spice goes in to many savoury dishes and replaces vanilla as the main flavouring of custard, ices and chocolate desserts. In Spain it is usually included in biscuits and cakes.

Canelones
Cannelloni, stuffed and covered in sauce. In Spain, they are sold as roll-them-yourself squares of pasta.

Canelones a la barcelonesa ✪✪
Cannelloni stuffed with ham and chicken livers (*foie gras* if you are lucky), in a tomato sauce and sherry sauce. They are then topped with béchamel sauce and grilled.

Cangrejo (de mar)
The large-clawed crab.

Cangrejos de rió ✪✪
Freshwater crayfish. Messy to eat, but very good, cooked with tomato, brandy and chilli.

Cantabria, queso de ✪
A flattish round cheese, semi-hard and made from cows' cream in a celebrated cheese area in the North.

Cañutillos de crema
Pastry custard horns.

A feast from land and sea

Cap roig
Scorpion fish. Can be baked if large, but is mostly used for soup; see ESCORPENA.

Capirotada, la ✪✪
Meat hidden by a 'hood' of almond sauce. The dish may be made from rabbit, chicken or other small birds and even meatballs.

Capitón
Type of grey mullet; see LISA.

Caqui
Kaki or persimmon, a winter tree fruit. Very acid unless it is soft, yellow and like an over-ripe tomato.

Carabineros ✪
Enormous, showy scarlet prawns with purplish heads, named for their military colouring. They are not as good value for money as LANGOSTINOS, being a bit bland, so their flavour is boosted with brandy. They are often made into soup.

Caracoles
Snails. A popular country food, often just served with vinegar. *Sin trabajo* means out of their shells – 'no work'!

Carajitos ✪✪
Hazelnut macaroons.

Caramelos
Sweets.

Carbonero
The black-backed coalfish, coley or saithe. Cooked like MERLUZA.

Cardamomo
Cardamom.

Cardo
Cardoon, related to the globe artichoke, though the stalks are blanched in plastic, rather like celery. These are eaten in white sauce, often with ham, or braised.

Cargolada, la ✪✪✪
A snail feast in Catalunya; *cargol* is a snail.

Cari
Curry.

Carn d'olla
See ESCUDELLA.

Carne
Meat; means beef without further description. *Carne de vaca* (cow) is the main Spanish beef, not of particular quality. *Carne de buey* (ox) also makes good beef stews.

Carne de buey en estofado ✪✪
A stew, usually with root vegetables. *A la catalana*, it may have BUTIFARRA (white sausage) and chocolate in it, and *con peras de castañas* is with pears, thickened with chestnuts.

Carne de lidia
Bull's meat. Dark red, tough and strong in flavour – not sold in ordinary butchers.

Carne picada
Minced meat.

Carnero
Mutton. Excellent *estofado* (braised) or *con ajo* (with garlic) for it has more flavour than young lamb.

Carnero verde ✪✪
Mutton dish from Tenerife. Braised with chopped parsley, mint and lettuce heart, with lemon juice and spices.

Carquinyolis
Almond biscuit, made hard by slicing the loaf and rebaking the slices. Its crumbs are used for thickening meat sauces.

Carrillada
Pig's cheek. Stewed in sherry in the south.

Cártamo
Safflower. The false saffron, bright yellow, but without the incomparable taste.

Casadielles ✪✪
Little sweet puff-pastry turnovers, filled with ground walnuts, then baked or fried.

Castañas
Chestnuts. They are made into a simple cream soup, flavoured with cinnamon, and are also cooked *con leche*, in milk, as a pudding with sugar.

Caza
The 'hunt' and so game.

Chorizo, cheese and fresh bread for a tasty snack – plus a glass of wine, of course

Cazón
The smooth-hound, one of the best edible sharks, because it feeds on shellfish. Its steaks are white, firm and somewhat dry.

Cazón en adobo ✪✪
Is marinated in paprika and vinegar, then battered and deep-fried. Good in Cádiz.

Cazuela
Spain's commonest brown cooking pot. It gives its name to any stew that comes out of it. Little *cazuelitas* are much used for cooking individual portions of fish – with plenty of sauce – and for eggs and mushrooms.

Cebolla
Onion. *Cebollone* is the Castilian for CALÇOT. *Cebolletas* are spring onions and *cebollinos*, chives. *Encebollada* means in onion sauce.

Cecina ✪✪
Dried beef eaten raw like ham, (what Americans call 'jerky'), *ceniza* in Catalunya. There is a tuna version.

Centeno
Rye. A black bread made in Galicia.

Centollo ✪✪✪
Spider crab. There is only meat enough for one person on each crab, for its claws are small and empty.
The flesh is stronger and sweeter than that of clawed crabs, so often mixed with hake, brandy, parsley, garlic and lemon and stuffed back in to the shell. This may be grilled.

Cerdo
Pork, the common meat.

Cerezas
Cherries.

Cervera, queso de ✪
A fresh ewes' milk cheese, made in Valencia.

Chacina
Minced pork or sausage filling. *Chacinería* are pork products – charcuterie.

Chalotas
Shallots.

Champiñones ✪
Cultivated mushrooms. Often served *al ajillo* (with garlic) like wild ones. They are good

rellenos, stuffed with sausage or pork and crumbs, or fried with ham.

Chanfaina ✪✪
A stew eaten on the day of pig killing, the *matanza*. It contains the lungs, lights, head, an other parts of the pig with the liver. However, do not confuse this with dishes such as *pollo en chanfaina*, which is chicken in SAMFAINA sauce.

Changurro, txangurro ✪✪✪
The Basque term for CENTOLLO, a popular *tapa* potted.

Chanquetes ✪✪
The over-fished gobies, slim silver fish, nicknamed 'sea spaghetti', and a Málaga speciality. This is now a term for any tiny fried fish, battered and deep-fried.

Cherna
Wreckfish or stone bass, a grouper. Cooked like MERO.

Chicarones
The crackling made from pork skin, left when fat is rendered. This is sold as a snack and is sometimes included in bread.

Chicarro
Coarse horse mackerel or scad. Best grilled.

Chipirones ✪✪✪
Tiny squid. Good when stuffed with their own tentacles and served in a sauce of their own ink (*en su tinta*).

Chirimoyas
Custard apples. Eat them with a spoon, spitting out the big seeds. They are very smooth and creamy when ripe.

Choco ✪✪
A small cuttlefish. Stewed *con habas* (with beans).

Chocolate
Chocolate is not good in Spain, except in the Basque country. Bars of chocolate are poor quality; only the breakfast drink is good.

Chocolate, marquesa de ✪
Chocolate mousse is flavoured with cinnamon or orange.

Chopa ✪✪
Red or black bream. Good to eat; see DENTÓN. Excellent *a la sidra* (in cider).

Chopitos
Small cuttlefish; see SEPIA.

Chorizo ✪✪✪
The scarlet sausage, flavoured with the

choricero (chilli), which is sweet but not very hot. There are two types of sausage. The fatter one is the equivalent of salami, eaten sliced on bread. The other is stewed with beans and soups, or fried, and comes hot or mild.

Choto ✪✪✪
Baby kid; see CABRA.

Chufa
Tiger nut. This is the tuber of a type of sedge. Made into the chilled drink HORCHATA, sometimes iced.

Chuletas de cerdo
Pork chops. Usually dusted with parprika and fried or grilled, then served with a little lemon juice.

Chuletas de cordero
Lamb chops. A luxury.

Chuletas de cordero a la navarra ✪✪
Lamb chops in a sauce of ham, onion and tomato.

Chuletas de cordero al sarmiento ✪✪✪
Tiny (and expensive) lamb chops, grilled over vine prunings.

Chuletas de ternera ✪✪
Veal chops, big and juicy. Best *a la riojana* (with roast red peppers).

Chuletón
An enormous wing rib beef chop. Beef is best in the north of Spain.

Chumbo ✪
Cactus fruit or prickly pear. Very refreshing. The trick is to peel them with knives and forks, avoiding spines.

Churros ✪✪
Breakfast fritters. These ubiquitous fritters are sold in every market. The dough is piped in circles into the hot fat before your eyes. The fritter rings may then be threaded onto a reed for carrying, and sugared. Good with breakfast chocolate or coffee.

Churrusco ✪✪
Means 'scorched', and so barbecued; often spare ribs.

Cidra
A big squash with stringy flesh. It is boiled in sugar to make a favourite jam; see CABELLO DE ANGEL.

Ciervo
Deer. The meat is tough, so best stewed with herbs.

Chocolate and churros, *a sugary treat for breakfast*

Cigalas ✪✪✪
Not to be missed, these are what the Italians call *scampi* and the English, Dublin Bay prawns. There is some meat in the claws, but most in the tail. Unlike other prawns, they are pink when raw. Eat them boiled or grilled, with coarse salt.

Cilantro, culantro
Coriander. Fresh leaves are used in the Canary Islands.

Ciruelas
Plums and greengages. *Ciruelas en aguardiente* are bottled in *eau-de-vie*.

Ciruelas pasas
Prunes. Very good soaked in anis.

Clavo
Cloves (literally nails).

Coca mallorquina ✪✪
Next cousin to the Italian pizza, with tomato and onions and often sausage on top – less often cheese. Sweet ones include currants or candied fruit.

Cochifrito a la navarra ✪✪✪
Milk-fed lamb stewed almost without vegetables, just lemon juice, garlic and paprika or saffron.

Cochinillo asado ✪✪✪
Suckling pig, roasted when it is so young and tender it can be carved with the edge of a plate.

Cocido
'Cooked' in Spain really means simmered. *Cocido de col* is simply simmered cabbage.

Cocido madrileño ✪✪✪
Meat dish of salt pork, beef and stewing hen, simmered in a pot with chick-peas. A second pot contains cabbage and CHORIZO. Sometimes PELOTAS (meat dumplings) are simmered too. The meal is served in two or three more courses. First the broth (*caldo*) with rice in it as soup, often the cabbage and sliced sausage second, and then the sliced meats and chick-peas (sometimes with tomato sauce or pickles) last. Every region in Spain has its own *cocido*, often with more vegetables. For example the Basques include red beans, while in the south they tend to be sweeter, with pumpkin or sweet potatoes – and every region includes its own local sausages.

Cocido madrileño, *Spain's national meat dish*

Coco
Coconut. *Cocos* or *cocados* are little coconut cakes.

Cóctel
Cocktail, as in *de mariscos* (seafood cocktail).

Cordonices
Wild quail. These are large and plump like French ones, not tiny farmed birds. See also POCHAS CON CORDONICES, ZURRÓN.

Cordonices al ajillo ✪✪
Quail, roast or pot roast with wine or garlic, often stuffed with their own gizzards.

Cordonices en hojas de parra ✪✪
Quail wrapped in vine leaves.

Cogollo
Means a 'core' or 'heart'. Often means quartered lettuce hearts, but also artichoke bases and *cogollo de palmito* (palm heart).

Col blanca
White cabbage. Served AJIACEITE, or *rellena* (stuffed).

Cola
Tail. *Cola de vaca* is oxtail; see RABO DE TORO.

Coliflor
Cauliflower.

Coliflor frita ✪
Marinated cauliflower, crumbed, or just egged, then fried.

Collejas
Lambs' lettuce or corn salad.

Colmenilla ✪
Morel mushrooms.

Comino
Cumin. Introduced by the Arabs, it has become a basic barbecue spice.

Compota
Cooked dried fruit.

Concha fina ✪✪✪
The big Venus shell clam, with a mahogany-coloured shell. It is eaten raw, with chilled FINO. Inside is a glory of scarlet and orange, hence the name 'fine shell'.

Concha peregrina
Scallop. Their shells are the badge of Santiago pilgrims; see VIERAS.

Conejo ✪✪
Rabbit; *del monte*, if it is wild. This popular food is commonly stewed (*guisado*) with onions, herbs and wine, or with cider in the north. A gravy with chocolate is common.

ATASCABURRA has plenty of garlic, CAPIROTADA has an almond sauce. Pies and cold jellied rabbit *al vinagreta*, or EN SALMOREJO, are also popular.

Conejo con caracoles ✪✪
A combination of snails and rabbit, both 'free food'. The snails feed on rosemary and so flavour the meat.

Congrio
Conger eel. Good with *salsa verde*; see MERLUZA.

Consomé al jerez ✪✪✪
Correctly *caldo* (broth) laced with sherry and the founder of a great tradition of clear soups.

Coques, coquetes
Flat breads; see COCA.

Coquinas ✪
Wedge shell clams. Eaten raw, or like ALMEJAS.

Corazón
Heart. Best stewed and often included in a lamb stew.

Cordero
Lamb. A luxury but it is rarely eked out with vegetables when stewed.

Cordero al chilindrón ✪✪✪
An Aragón speciality of lamb stewed with red peppers.

Cordero al pastor ✪✪✪
Stewed lamb, seasoned with a little garlic and saffron and a sauce thickened with its own liver.

Cordero asado ✪✪✪
Roast lamb. At its best from a baker's oven. The very best are *cordero lechal* or *mamón* (suckling lamb).

Cordero asado a la manchega ✪✪
Lamb roasted in an earthenware dish with garlic and onions.

Corvina
Meagre (fish). Good to eat fried, or cooked like LUBINA.

Corzo
Roe deer.

Costellada ✪✪
Lamb chops grilled over an open fire with BUTIFARRA.

37

Costillas a la parilla ✪✪
Spare ribs grilled or baked (*al horno*). Excellent with ALIOLI.

Costra
Means 'crust'. So with cheese (*costrada manchego*) it becomes toasted cheese.

Costrada
Can be a pastry slice (or a *millefeuilles*) with custard and fruit, or a slice of cake with a candied top.

Costrada navarra ✪✪
A layered soup of CHORIZO or bread and vegetables, soaked in broth then baked with eggs on top to make a crust. This is a common way of presenting thick soups.

Crema
A purée soup; can be sweet.

Crema catalana ✪✪✪
Cream dessert. The custard is strongly flavoured with cinnamon and lemon zest, then fiercely grilled with a minute amount of sugar. The result is a net of caramel and a slight taste of the grill. This *crème brûlée* is served very cold.

Crema de San José ✪✪
A chilled egg custard; see NATILLAS.

Cremadina
A custard filling – French *crème pâtissière*.

Creme catalana, one of Spain's great cream desserts

Cremat
Catalan for 'burned'. It is used for their wonderful pudding and for flamed coffee. *Pescado al cremat* means fish in 'burnt garlic' sauce: really cooked to a rich golden brown.

Criadillas
Testicles, made into fritters.

Criadillas de la tierra
Truffles; see TRUFA.

Croquetas ✪✪
Deep-fried croquettes. A popular *tapa*, they are made of minced meat, bound with egg, or based on béchamel sauce, egged, crumbed and fried. These are also delicious made with BACALAO, shrimps (*quisquillas*) or spinach (*espinacas*).

Cru de peix ✪✪
Literally 'raw fish', a quick-cooked fish stew with saffron and paprika.

Crudo
Raw. *Para comer crudo* means to eat raw.

Cuajada con miel ✪✪
Junket (very like yoghurt). Sold in little straight-sided earthenware pots and eaten with honey, and also made into a cheesecake. *Cuajo* is rennet, that curdles the milk.

Culantro, cilantro
Coriander.

D

Dátiles
Palm dates – a super-sweet fresh fruit.

Delicias
A little *tapa* biscuit or spongecake. For *delicias de hojaldre*, see PALMERAS.

Dentón ✪✪✪
Dentex (fish), a bream with pinkish tints. It makes very good eating, especially grilled or baked with onion (*al horno*). Little and lesser breams tend to end up in soup.

Despojos
Offal.

Dorada
The best and most expensive of the breams, called a gilt-head because of its golden eyebrow.

Dorada a la sal ✪✪✪
Dorada baked completely encrusted with salt, then hammered open at the table. A party dish and a Murcian speciality.

Dulce
Means 'sweet', and hence is used for sweets. Stiff cold fruit pastes such as *dulce de membrillo* (quince) are common, and also desserts like *dulce malagueño*, semolina with egg yolks, sugar, raisins and quince.

Duquesa ✪
A pie shaped like a little English pork pie, it may contain fish or vegetables. *Duquesitas* are smaller and sweet.

E

Eglefino
Haddock. Found smoked but rarely fresh.

Emborrachada
'Drunken', so marinated or in wine sauce.

Embutido
A fresh sausage; literally 'stuffed'. Home-made, it is *a la casera*.

Empanada de lomo ✪
Pork loin and pepper pie, called *de raxó* in Galicia. Pies are also made of fish, such as the skinny, yellow-fleshed *xouba* and *de vieieras* (scallop pie); others are made of BACALAO.

Empanada de Pascua ✪✪
Easter pie of young lamb.

Empankdillos ✪✪
Small savoury pies. Tuna and tomato are good and rather spicy if they are *murciana*, or they may be pork or ham with spinach. The dough is sold ready-cut in packets. The name includes sweet doughnuts, which may contain jam – CIDRA.

Empanados/...das
Means 'breaded' and then fried, for example cutlets.

Emparador
Swordfish; see PEZ ESPADA.

Emparedado
Sandwiched, literally 'enfolded'. The sandwich is soaked in milk, then fried and served hot (*caliente*).

Empedrada, la ✪✪
This 'speckled' dish is a Catalan salted cod salad with broad beans.

Encargo, por
Made to order.

Endibia
Chicory (in white heads).

Enebro
Juniper berry.

Eneldo
Dill.

Ensaimada ✪✪
A delicious sweet yeast roll in a spiral, served for breakfast in Mallorca. Larger ones, the size of pizzas, may be topped with slices of SOBRASADA (red pork sausages).

Ensalada ✪
Salad. The best-known salad is crisp lettuce, onion rings and olives, perhaps with tomato slices. However, *ensalada mixta* in a larger restaurant is likely to be an elaborate mixture of vegetables. Other possibilities are *lechuga* (lettuce), *tomate* (tomato), *de habas* (cooked beans), perhaps dressed with mint, and seasonal salad (*del tiempo*). They are accompanied by oil and vinegar, to dress yourself.

Ensalada de San Isidro ✪✪
This salad named after the saint of Madrid contains lettuce with marinated ATÚN (tuna).

Ensaladilla ✪✪
Means 'little' or Russian salad, a mixture of cooked, diced potato with peas, carrots and artichoke bases in mayonnaise.

Catalan salad

Entrecot a la pimienta ✪✪
Steak with peppercorns, *not* chopped vegetable peppers.

Entremés variados
Assorted appetizers. *De carne* is a selection of sliced meats.

Erizos de mar
Hedgehog sea urchins. They are broken and eaten with a spoon like a boiled egg, combined with scrambled egg, or used for a creamy sauce.

Escabeche
Pickled by cooking in wine and vinegar. Fish, meat and vegetables like aubergines are all cooked this way, then left until cold. *Escabechado* means pickled.

Escaldums ✪✪
Chicken or turkey pieces are panfried, then finished in an onion and tomato sauce, thickened with almonds and SOBRASADA sausage.

Escalivada ✪✪✪
A delicious salad of cold, baked vegetables, like aubergines and peppers, dressed with virgin olive oil and sometimes anchovies. The name means 'barbecued'. Tomatoes may be included too. The vegetables may be puréed and served chilled.

Escaloña
Shallot.

Escarola
Endive.

Escorpena, escorpión
Scorpion fish. Mostly used for fish soups, but the flesh (under the venomous spines) is good if served filleted.

Escudella i carn d'olla ✪✪✪
The Catalan COCIDO of boiled meat. It includes ham, chicken, cubed veal, BUTIFARRA and dried and fresh vegetables. The broth is served first, then the meat and vegetables. *Escudella de pagès*, is 'country style', with carrots, potatoes and cabbage.

Espada, pez
Swordfish. *Filetes* are good grilled. See also PEZ ESPADA.

Espadín
A sprat; whitebait if they are very small.

Espaldilla
Shoulder of beef. Good pot-roast.

Espárragos con dos salsas ✪✪
White canned asparagus with vinaigrette served with mayonnaise or a sauce of chopped tomato.

Espárragos trigueros or amargueros ✪✪✪
Wild (bitter) asparagus, which once 'grew among the wheat'. A spring speciality, best with scrambled eggs (REVUELTOS), it is also sautéed or baked with crumbs.

Especias
Spices. Spanish spices date from Moorish times. Cinnamon (*canela*), appears in many savoury dishes. *Comino* (cumin) was liked by the Moors and is a main ingredient in the spice mix *pinchitos morunos*. In specialist shops, mixtures are sold for tripe, snails, fish and for *adobos de carne* – meat marinades. *Colorante* is also sold to dye PAELLA yellow.

Espeto, al
Cooked on a spit.

Espinacas
Spinach. It makes soup with GARBANZOS (chick-peas) and is stewed in a mixed MENESTRA.

Espinacas a la catalana ✪✪
Spinach tossed in butter with anchovy, pine nuts and raisins.

Esquiexada ✪✪✪
A Catalan starter salad of slivers of red pepper, tomato and raw salted cod.

Estofado
This does not mean stuffed, but braised. *Estofado de buey* is beef stew. It will include roots like carrot and turnips in the northwest, and potatoes in the south. *Estofado a la catalana* may contain chocolate.

Estornino
Spanish mackerel, with pinkish oily flesh. Of good quality, so some people prefer it to CABALLA (common mackerel).

Estragón
Tarragon.

F

Faba, fave
A large buttery-textured dried bean. Normally stewed with garlic and paprika.

Fabada asturiana ✪✪✪
A famous slow-cooked bean dish in Asturias, with ham and salt pork and made spicy with saffron, MORCILLAS and CHORIZO.

Fabes a la granja ✪✪
Spain's top white beans: *al la granja* indicates a superior dish.

Faisán
Pheasant.

Faisán a las uvas ✪✪
Pot-roasted pheasant in port, served with grapes.

Faisán al modo de Alcántara ✪✪✪
Europe's most celebrated game dish: pheasant stuffed with its own liver and truffles. It is marinated, roasted and served with truffle and port sauce. The recipe was discovered in a Spanish monastery by a looting Napoleonic army and promoted by French chef Escoffier.

Falda rellena
Stuffed flank.

Faramallas
Sweet fritter in Galicia.

Farro
This vegetable soup takes its name from pearl barley, but sometimes it contains vermicelli instead.

Faves, fabes
Beans. Used for FABADA in Asturias, but also eaten in the south in vegetable stews like *faves al tombet* ; see TUMBET.

Fesol
Type of dried bean.

Fiambre
Cold pressed meat (though a *fiambre de bonito* is made from tuna). *Fiambre de ternera* is veal pâté.

Fideos
Vermicelli. Now sold in a variety of thicknesses. They are popular in soups.

Fideuà a la mariscos ✪✪✪
A wonderful shellfish PAELLA – but made with FIDEOS, not rice.

Filete
A fillet – of beef or fish.

Filloas ✪✪
Large crêpes, cooked on a griddle like the Breton ones, jam- or custard-filled.

Flamenquines ✪✪
Originally rolled-up ham and cheese, deep-fried as a *tapa*. The more sophisticated versions may include pork or be enclosed in béchamel and a crumb coating before frying.

Flan de huevos ✪✪✪
Moulded caramel custard and Spain's national sweet, which is excellent if *a la casa* (home made). *Flan de naranja* is made from orange juice.

Flaó, flaón
Sweet cheesecake, often flavoured with anis. Tiny ones are pastries with curd cheese.

Flores　　　　　　　　　　　　✪✪
Sweet fritters, made in the west. They may be 'flower-shaped' (*de manchego*) and are sprinkled with honey or sugar.

Frambuesas
Raspberries.

Francesa, a la
In the French style, that is, with a white sauce.

Frejol
Type of dried bean.

Fresas
Strawberries. Usually without cream. Delicious *con anis* or with OLOROSO sherry.

Fricadelas
Meat patties.

Fricandó　　　　　　　　　　　　✪
Small pieces of beef or veal, fried, then finished in a sauce.

Frijoles
Dried beans. In the Canary Islands, black beans and rice are *frijoles con arroz*.

Frío
Cold.

Who can resist ripe strawberries?

Frito
Fried, so *fritos* are fritters. A fried dish, *frite de cordero*, is excellent made with young lamb. *Fritillos* (little fritters) may be sweet.

Fritura de pescado　　　　　　✪✪✪
A fry-up of mixed fish; *fritura a la gaditana* or *malagueña* are deliciously crisp.

Frixuelos　　　　　　　　　　　　✪
Sweet pancakes served with honey.

Fruta
Fruit. Some less familiar fruit worth trying, all of them half-wild in Spain, are figs (*higos*), pomegranates (*granadas*) and prickly pears (*chumbos*).

Frutas de Aragón　　　　　　　　✪
Crystallised fruits which are then chocolate-coated.

Fuerte
Highly spiced, possibly with added vinegar. 'Something stronger' (*más fuerte*) means alcoholic if applied to drinks. *Fuerte* means bitter or unripe, if applied to fruit.

G

Gachas
Gruel. A survivor from medieval times, made with wheat or other flours (like GOFIO). It can be milky and sweet (with aniseed and lemon) or flavoured with garlic and ham. In some places it is so thick that it sets when cold (like porridge) and slabs are then fried. There is a garlic and potato version in the south.

Galets, sopa de　　　　　　　　✪
Galets are small pasta, and this pleasant soup also contains small meatballs. It is flavoured with fresh celery leaves.

Galletas
Any crisp biscuits.

Gallina
Hen, suggesting a well-stewed chicken dish.

Gallineta
Norway haddock (also called bluemouth and red fish) and related to rascasse. Famous for soups. Its firm flesh is good cooked like bream; see DENTÓN.

Gallo
A popular flatfish. It is best plain fried with plenty of lemon juice squeezed over.

Galludo
Dogfish or small shark. Good to eat; see cazón.

Gamba
One of the best prawns, sold raw in Spain. Needs 2 or 3 minutes cooking in boiling water.

Gambas con gabardinas ✪✪✪
'Prawns in mackintoshes', battered then deep-fried until crisp; a popluar *tapa*.

Gambas pil-pil ✪✪✪
Prawns sizzling in oil and garlic, made very hot with chilli. Mop the juice up with your bread (see recipe page 111). The dish has no relation to the BACALAO of the same name. In the south, it is sometimes called *piri-piri* after a similar Portuguese dish.

Ganso
Goose, see also OCA.

Garbanzos
Chick-peas, potatoes of Spain. They need soaking, then 1 to 1 ½ hours' simmering. The equivalent of crisps are *salteados*, nutty and ready-sautéed as a snack, or toasted (TORRADOS). *En remojo* in a market, means 'soaked' for cooking. *Refritos* means boiled and fried in a new dish.

Garbanzos con espinacas ✪
A pleasant stew of chick-peas, spinach and garlic, perhaps with tomato and peppers.

Garbanzos y chorizo ✪✪✪
The perfect combination of nutty chick-peas with spicy sausage to flavour them.

Garbure navarro ✪
A Spanish version of a French soup, with a mixture of vegetables and salt pork, and probably CHORIZO.

Garrapiñadas
See ALMENDRAS.

Gatavask ✪✪
Also called *gâteau basque* and *pastel vasco*, this is a heavy sweet-pastry tart, with set custard, jam or fruit inside. Excellent for picnics.

Gazpacho ✪✪✪
The famed chilled soup is made from puréed bread and garlic, with raw peppers, tomato and cucumber, made creamy with oil and vinegar; this is labelled *sevillana, andaluz* or *rojo*. The Madrid version includes mayonnaise. In winter it is served hot (*caliente*).

Cold and colourful – the famous Spanish Gazpacho

Gazpacho blanco ✪✪✪
A creamy white version of GAZPACHO, based on garlic, vinegar and almonds *con uvas* (with muscat grapes).

Gazpacho manchego ✪✪
A rich mixed game pâté. The liquid is thickened with breadcrumbs like *gazpacho* soup, which explains the name.

Gazpachuelo ✪✪
A creamy soup, served just warm, based on mayonnaise, sometimes thinned with fish soup. It may contain potatoes and their cooking water. The connection with GAZPACHO is the vinegar in it.

Gelats
Catalan for ices. Try the *gelat d'amentilla* (almond sorbet) in Mallorca.

Giraboix ✪✪
A salted cod stew with vegetables, including green beans and cabbage, as well as potatoes, served with ALIOLI. The highly-seasoned broth can be served as soup starter.

Girasol
Sunflower. Unripe black seeds are crushed to make a bland cooking oil. The white seeds are eaten as a snack.

Glorias
A little sweet pastry (sometimes a meringue) with an almond or sweet potato filling.

Gofio
Toasted cornmeal. In the Canary Islands, this is made into balls as a substitute for bread.

Golosina
A sweet titbit.

Granada ✪
Pomegranate. The fruit is hard outside and crammed with red seeds inside. Soak it in hot water to make it easier to peel. Swallow or spit out the tiny seed enclosed in each capsule of juice, as you please. *Granadina* may be a syrup of the juice.

Granadina
Grenadine, the yellow passion fruit. Or see above.

Granizado ✪
A grainy fruit sorbet or, sometimes, iced drink: the Spanish version of the Italian *granita*. The Catalan is *granissat*.

Gratinado
Au gratin.

Greixera ✪
A Mallorcan casserole. There are meat ones,

and layered vegetable and egg ones, like *greixera d'ous*. One is like a quiche filling without the pastry. Desserts are made too, all in the shallow round-bottomed casserole, the *greixonera*.

Greixera al llagosta ✪✪✪
Lobster gratin, with a spinach and egg sauce.

Greixonera de brossat ✪
A cheesecake in Mallorca, made with REQUESÓN. Less commonly, a baked bread-and-milk pudding,

Grelos
The spring leaves and flower buds of turnip tops, stewed; see LACÓN CON GRELOS.

Grosellas
Red or black currants.

Guinda
Cocktail or glacé cherry.

Guindilla
The one hot chilli in the Spanish kitchen, found in cold Galicia. The name means 'cherry-red'. They are used for cooking, and sold dried as *rama*, and pickled in jars.

Guirlache ✪✪
A hard toffee containing toasted almonds and aniseeds.

Guisado
Stewed. This may be a stew of vegetables alone, eg *guiso de espárragos amargueros* (stew of wild asparagus).

Guisantes ✪
Peas. Often stewed with ham *a la española*, or tomatoes, and included in MENESTRA and many veal dishes.

Guiso de trigo ✪
Historic soup with wheat grains, and usually chick-peas and turnips too.

H

Habas
Fresh or dried broad beans. *A la catalana* is beans cooked with TOCINO (pork fat) and BUTIFARRA. *Ensalada* is a bean salad which includes mint.

Habas con jamón ✪✪✪
Fresh broad beans combined with fried ham, parsley and hard-boiled eggs. It is also called *habas españolas, rondeña* and *a la granadina*.

Habichuelas
Green summer beans.

Hamburguesa
Hamburgers. In Spain, they are made of minced pork, and pork and beef mixtures, as well as all beef.

Harina
Flour.

Helado
Ice-cream is sold in the usual European flavours: *de vainilla*, *de chocolate* and *de limón*, all of which you can guess. Strawberry is *de fresas*. The most popular ice-cream in Spain, which accompanies fruit salad, etc, is *canela* (cinnamon), which also makes an unusual sorbet. Other unusual Spanish ices are *moscatel* (muscat grapes) and *turrón* (nougat). A *copa* is a sundae, while a *tarta helada* is an ice-cream with a sponge layer. An ice-cream cone is *un cucurucho*.

Pomegranate, full of red-jewelled seeds

Helado quemado ✪
Ice-cream in a pot, topped with grilled sugar.

Hervido
Poached, from *hervir* (to bubble or boil).

Hierba buena
The 'good herb' is mint. Its use dates back to the Arabs.

Hierba Luisa
Lemon verbena.

Higadillos, higiditos
Chicken livers. *Salteados* are sautéed, and they are much used with rice and eggs.

Hígado de ternera ✪✪
Calf's liver. *Con cebolla* is with fried onion and often ham. *Hígado guisado* is stewed lamb's livers with onions and potatoes.

Higos
Figs.

Hinojo
Fennel. Wild in Spain, it is added to fish and used for salad.

Hojaldre
Layered like 'leaves', and so puff pastry. The Spanish version is a bit heavy. Ususally it is sweet, for example cream slices, but *hojaldre de salmón* is salmon pie.

45

THE VERSATILE EGG

As well as the basic cooking methods, eggs are treated as a separate course in Spain. They may be added to many vegetable, pork or game mixtures, or have additions like prawns or chopped tomato. An egg may be *pasado por agua*, boiled – when it will be very soft and served in a wine glass. You peel it, drop it back in and eat with a spoon. *Huevos estrellados* are fried and sunny side up, *escalfados* are poached and *fritos* fried or deep-fried; the latter are puffy and excellent.

✪✪✪ **Huevos a la flamenca** An egg dish of many colours, hence the name. A tomato and vegetable sauce then goes in a casserole, then the eggs, which may be topped with ham, CHORIZO and prawns, before baking (see recipe page 102).
✪ **Huevos a la gitanilla** Gypsy eggs, baked in a purée of bread, almonds ground with cumin, and garlic.
Huevos rellenos Popular stuffed hard-boiled eggs, often with tuna or anchovy (de anchoa).

Hojas de parra
Vine leaves. Served stuffed with minced meat and bread, or wrapped round birds such as quail.

Hongos ✪✪
The wild mushrooms that grow around tree stumps. Excellent with crêpes or eggs. *A la Andaluza* they are cooked with sherry or Málaga wine. Never pick your own, buy them from the markets.

Horchata ✪
Tiger nut drink, sometimes an ice-cream; see CHUFA.

Hornazo
A 'baked' Easter cake, decorated with eggs, and sometimes containing sausage.

Horno
Oven.

Hortelana
The adjective 'vegetable' from *huerta* (the 'vegetable plot'). It often indicates vegetables as garnish, which is uncommon in Spain.

Huesos
Bones.

Huesos de santo
'Saint's bones', for All Saints. Once these were deep-fried potato pastries, stuffed with custard, but now they are made of marzipan.

Huevas
Fish roes. Often *aliñadas* (marinated) or *fritas*, made into crisp fritters.

Huevas prensadas ✪✪
Salted pressed tuna roe.

Huevo
Egg (see box above).

I

Idiazábal, queso de ✪✪
Pride of the Basque country, this hard pressed ewes' milk cheese is shaped like a small drum. Smoked ones are stronger, with toffee-coloured rinds.

Intxaursalsa ✪✪✪
A Basque walnut cream, eaten chilled on Christmas Eve.

J

Jabalí ✪✪
Boar, found in north and southern Spain. *Estofado* (stewed) and *a la montañesa* both mean with herbs and onion.

Jamón
For Spain's famous raw ham see SERRANO. Cooked ham on the bone is called *jamón de York*. Lean slices are often called MAGRO. Lesser hams are made with shoulder (*fiambre de paleta*).

Jamón al jerez ✪✪
Braised ham in sherry.

Jamón con melón o higos ✪
Sliced ham with melon or figs.

Japuta
Pomfret (fish). An excellent fish – though this name means 'son of a bitch'; see PALOMETA.

Jarabe ✪✪
Syrup made from fresh fruit. Excellent over crushed ice.

Jarrete de ternera
A shin bone of veal made into some tasty stews.

Jibia ✪✪
Another name for cuttlefish, see SEPIA. Excellent *en salsa* – in a sauce with saffron and cumin.

Judías
Dried beans. *Judías pintas* ('painted beans') are the speckled brown borlotti beans.

Judías a lo tío Lucas ✪✪✪
A popular Madrid dish of mildly spiced beans. The Uncle Luke of the title invented it in Cádiz to feed the half-starved sailors waiting to be paid off at the end of voyages.

Judías verdes
Green beans. *Con salsa de tomate* are with tomato sauce, *con jamón*, with ham. They are cooked with TOCINO and CHORIZO in Madrid.

Julivert
The lovely Catalan word for parsley.

Jurel
Horse mackerel (fish), related to CHICHARRO.

K

Kokotxas, cocochas ✪✪✪
Triangular throat pieces from the hake, and a Basque speciality. Delicious as tiny fritters

(fritas), they also garnish fish dishes, but are a bit gelatinous cooked with oil and garlic as *pil-pil*.

Koskera
See MERLUZA A LA VASCA.

L

Lacón con grelos ✪✪✪
A hearty Galician soup-stew of cured pork knuckle with the young leaf tops and flower buds or turnips, plus new potatoes.

Lamprea
Lamprey (fish).

Langosta ✪✪
The tiny-clawed rock lobster, called crawfish in Britain and crayfish in the US. Often served cold with mayonnaise; it is served hot in a spicy tomato sauce *al estilo de Bilbao*, or in rice.

Langosta a la Costa Brava ✪✪✪
Crawfish in tomato sauce flavoured with sweet RANCIO wine and brandy, and thickened with almonds and hazelnuts.

Langosta con pollo ✪✪✪
A Catalan mixture of lobster and chicken, in a SOFRITO-based tomato stew, thickened with a PICADA.

Hot and tasty – huevos a la flamenca

Langostinos ✪✪✪
Big deep-water prawns. Perhaps the best prawn – boiled or cooked simply *a la plancha* (on the hot iron) and served dressed *a la vinagreta* or with pungent ALIOLI. They are also cooked in white wine (*a la marinera*).

Laurel, hojas de
Bay leaves.

Lebrada de progonaos ✪✪
Stewed hare in wine. Like the French *civet*, it includes the animal's blood, but in Spain the sauce is thickened with pine nuts.

Lechal, lechazo ✪✪✪
A milk-fed lamb. A glory when roasted.

Leche, arroz con ✪✪
Cold, milky rice pudding, flavoured with lemon zest. A speciality in the northwest. Sometimes it has a grilled sugar topping (*quemado*).

Leche frita ✪✪
Literally 'fried milk', these hot or cold squares of stiff custard are creamy inside, with a crisp crust from being egg-and-crumbed, then fried. Found in the north.

Langostinos, *deep-water prawns in garlic, a popular Canarian dish*

Lechecillas de ternera ✪✪
Calves sweetbreads. Popularly made into a stew that may also include the liver and lights.

Lechona asada ✪✪✪
Roast suckling pig.

Lechuga
Lettuce. Usually a salad, but also cooked. *Cogollos* (hearts) may be floured and fried, and are sometimes mixed with other hot vegetables.

Legumbres
Pulses, fresh or dried.

Lengua
Tongue in the singular will be an ox tongue, in the plural, lambs' tongues.

Lengua estofada ✪✪
Braised tongue with vegetables, served hot. In Mallorca, pomegranate juice may be included.

Lenguado ✪✪
Sole, small and big. It is fried simply, coated with flour or crumbs, for example *a la gaditana*. In Madrid and the Basque country, it is often paired with wine and mushrooms; in Andalucía, where tiny single person ones are common, with tomatoes and peppers.

Lentejas
Lentils. They are made into soups (*sopa*) or stewed (*cocido*). *A la zamorana*, they are cooked with MORCILLA, garlic and paprika.

Levadura
Both baking powder and yeast.

Liadillos
'Tied up', and so stuffed meat or cabbage rolls.

Liebre ✪✪
Hare. Mostly *guisada* or *en su salsa* (stewed with herbs). Red wine is a common addition, with nutmeg, and the sauce is thickened with the liver.

Lima
Lime.

Limanda
Lemon sole.

Limón
Lemon.

Lisa ✪✪✪
Grey mullet, considered by the Spanish to be the best grey mullet Eat it grilled or baked, for it is fairly oily, but has a good flavour and is easy to bone. It is often cooked like LUBINA and is excellent with saffron sauce (*en amarillo*), on the south coast.

Liscos
A TORTILLA made with streaky bacon.

Llagosta a la catalana ✪✪✪
A Catalan lobster dish with a sauce of peppers, tomato, wine and brandy. Sometimes it includes chocolate and almonds.

Llampuga
Catalan for DORADA.

Llauna, a la
Catalan for 'in a metal oven dish', or baked.

Llegumet ✪✪✪
A thick dish with beans, rice *and* potatoes, in Alicante, including snails.

Locha
Small cod or loach.

Locro
Stewed with maize.

Lombarda ✪
Red cabbage. Cooked a *San Isidro* is with bacon and potatoes, or with apples and wine.

Lomo
Loin. Notably pork loin, much eaten in Spain. It may be pot roasted with sherry or sweet Málaga wine, or stuffed (*relleno*) with nuts, ham or SOBRASADA sausage.

Lomo bajo
Sirloin or loin of beef.

Lomo de cerdo a la zaragozana ✪
Pork loin cooked with ham, onions, wine and tomatoes, and the local chopped black olives.

Lomo de cerdo con leche ✪✪
Pork loin pot-roast in milk.

Lomo embuchado ✪✪✪
Smoked, pink pork loin cured whole in a sausage casing. It tastes like good ham. A *caña de lomo* is also a cured loin.

Longaniza ✪
A sausage, remarkable for its length, and sometimes fresh. Also a rather bland, hard, thin salami sausage, which hangs in a hank, wrapped around a wooden rod.

Lonja
Thick slice.

Lubina ✪✪✪
Sea bass. One of the finest fish, best when line-caught. Baked *Costa Brava* style with red wine and onions, poached or grilled, it is exceptional. *A la asturiana* it is cooked in cider (or white wine) with clams or mussels and possibly potatoes.

Lubina Albufera ✪✪✪
From the great Valencian freshwater lake, this sea bass is served with ground almond and paprika sauce.

Lucio
Pike.

M

Macarrones
Macaroni. Served with cheese sauce, and also chicken giblet dressing.

Macedonia de frutas
Fruit salad.

Machacón ✪✪
Boiled potatoes dressed with chopped tomato and pepper, plus oil and usually cumin.

Macis
Mace (part of nutmeg).

Maduro
Ripe.

Magdalenas
Sponge cup cakes, from the French *madeleines*.

Magro ✪✪
'Lean', usually pork. *Magro con tomate* is fried ham in tomato sauce. It is also served in sweet sauces of Málaga wine, or with cherries.

Mahón, queso de ✪✪
A well-regarded, flattish square cheese, semi-hard with a tangy taste. It is made from cows' milk in Menorca.

Mahonesa, mayonesa
Two words for mayonnaise, the first reflecting the belief it was invented at Mahón (Maó) on Menorca.

Maiz
Maize or sweetcorn.

Málaga, queso de ✪
A goats' milk cheese, matured for just five days.

Mamia
Basque junket; see CUAJADA.

Manchego, queso ✪✪✪
Spain's cheddar cheese. Made from ewes' milk, it is sold at various stages from semi-hard, when it is mild, to *añejo* (aged) which is sharp, hard and reminiscent of Parmesan. The waxed rind bears the mark of the rope

mould and the black drum form is best known, though some rinds are yellowish; colour does not indicate age.

Mandarina
Tangerine.

Manos de cerdo, manitas ✪
Trotters. They are cooked until the fat jellies, with beans or chick-peas (*con judías o garbazos*) to absorb the fat. For *manitas rehogadas*, they are boned out and stuffed, then egged, crumbed and fried.

Manteca colorá ✪✪
Paprika-flavoured pork fat. A bread spread that may also include shreds of meat, like French *rillettes*; a good starter.

Mantecados ✪✪
Rich, crumbly little 'lardy cakes' that often include ground almonds. The ones from Astorga in León are famous.

Mantequilla
Butter.

Manzana
Apple.

Manzanas asadas ✪
Baked apples or *rellenas* (stuffed), good if the stuffing is chestnut.

Manzanillas
Common small green olives.

Mar y tierra/mar y montana ✪✪✪
Dishes that combine the fish from the 'sea' with chicken from the 'mountain'. The most glamorous of these is chicken with lobster in a saffron, hazlenut and chocolate sauce.

Maragota
Wrasse (fish). With coarse and somewhat insipid flesh, it mainly goes in soups. It can be stuffed and baked (*al horno*).

Margarina
Margarine.

Mariscos
Shellfish.

Marmitako ✪✪✪
Basque shipboard stew, which takes its name from the cooking pot (the French *marmite*). It is made from BONITO (white tuna) and whole new potatoes in a piquant, puréed red pepper sauce.

Marrajo
Porbeagle shark. Good grilled; see CAILÓN

Marrón glacés ✪✪
Much more sugary than the crystallised French chestnuts.

Maruca
Spanish ling and the largest member of the cod family. It cooks more like whiting, so needs pepping up.

Masa
Bread dough or pastry.

Mata mulo
Very fresh. Literally 'the mule killer', it refers to the speed with which fish is rushed inland.

Mataero, ajo de ❂
A very similar dish to MORTERUELO, with pork, bacon, liver and pine kernels.

Matalahuva/matalahuga
Aniseed (aniseed plant).

Matanza ❂❂❂
A big event in the peasant food year, when the pig is killed by a *matador*, some time in November after All Saints. The sequence of dishes starts with the liver and brains on the first day, which make a splendid meal! Many sausages are made with the offal and blood.

Mató
Fresh goats' milk cheese.

Mazapán ❂
Marzipan. It is made into *figuritas*, little animals, shapes and Christmas figures.

Mejillones ❂❂❂
Mussels. They are often included in fish sauces, soups and PAELLA. They are served cold on the shell (*a la vinagreta*) or baked (*al horno*), they are also good fried in bread-crumbs (*empanados*).

Meijillones a la marinera ❂❂
Mussels opened in white wine with onion, garlic and oil.

Mejorana
Marjoram. Sweeter than oregano.

Mel i mató ❂❂
Fresh cream cheese served with honey (MIEL).

Melaza
Molasses.

Melindres
'Lady-finger' biscuits, sometimes marzipan.

Melocotón
Peach.

Melocotón en almíbar ❂❂
Peaches in syrup, from Arab times.

Melocotón asados en vino tinto ❂❂❂
Peaches baked in red wine.

Melón
Melon. Honeydews and Piel de Sapo are celebrated.

Melón con jamón ❂❂❂
Melon with raw SERRANO ham.

Membrillo ❂❂❂
Quince. Popular as a stewed fruit, but most of all as a stiff, sweet, pink paste, sold as *dulce*, *flan* or even *carne de membrillo*; good with hard cheese.

Menestra de Tuleda ❂❂❂
Asparagus stewed with other vegetables.

Menestra de verduras ❂
A vegetable stew. At its most attractive when it is a mixture of boiled with fried vegetables. Chopped hard-boiled eggs are added, and many versions include ham. *Menestra a la asturiana* includes fried potatoes and ham, while *extremeña* is based on potatoes and greens. *Menestra de pollo* includes chicken.

Manjar blanco ❂❂
Means 'white eat' and is a creamy ground almond dessert with lemon juice. It once included pounded chicken breasts.

Menta
Mint.

Menudillos
Chicken giblets. Common in rice dishes, baked with eggs and in tomato sauce.

Menudos
Offal.

Menudos gitanos
Gypsy tripe, cooked with ham, chick-peas, garlic, saffron and cumin, also called *callos a la andaluza*.

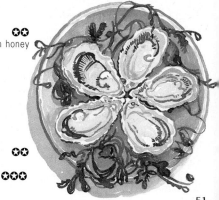

Merengues
Meringues.

Merlano
Whiting. A light, white rather tasteless fish.

Merlo
Wrasse (fish). Used in soup.

Merluza ✪✪✪
Hake. Spain's most popular and plentiful fish: fine-flavoured and flaky. It is cooked in cider (*a la sidra*), with capers (*alcaparras*), with potatoes (*gallega*) and is good cold (*con mayonesa*).

Merluza a la vasca ✪✪
Hake with white wine sauce, clams and prawns and sometimes asparagus tips or eggs (see recipe page 105).

Merluza en salsa verde ✪✪✪
Hake in a sauce made green with parsley. It has an onion base and contains clams, prawns and KOKOTXAS. Other names include *merluza bilbaina* and *cazuela Santander.*

Mermelada
A thick, compote-like jam of any flavour. Try peach or plum jam; berries are less good. Marmalade is *mermelada de naranja.*

Mero ✪✪✪
Grouper (fish). One of Spain's most delicious fish, it is lean and flaky. A versatile fish, it is good *al horno*, baked with white wine and

Catalan Mussels served in marine sauce

potatoes, grilled, or served hot in orange sauce, and cold, *en vinagreta.*

Michirones ✪✪
Broad beans stewed with CHORIZO and chilli.

Miel
Honey. Best from one flower, like orange flower (*miel de azahar*).

Mielga
Spur dog shark. One of the best edible sharks; see CAILÓN.

Miera cielo ✪✪
A roast red pepper salad, with slivers of dry roast salted cod in olive oil.

Migas ✪✪✪
Fried breadcrumbs or small croûtons. They give texture to many egg, bacon and vegetable dishes and make a dessert with chocolate sauce or grapes.

Migas canas
A savoury bread pudding of MIGAS with milk, and often bacon.

Mijo
Millet.

Modroñes
Arbutus. The fruit of the strawberry tree, pretty but not particularly good to eat.

Moixernon ✪
The earliest wild mushroom – 'St George's'.

Mojama ✪✪
The dark, salted back of the blue fin tuna. It is a luxury.

Mojarra

The two-banded bream. Excellent grilled or baked; see DENTÓN.

Mojete ✪✪

A simple salad of strips of cold roasted onions and peppers, dressed with lemon juice, garlic and oil, and sometimes cumin. Salted cod or sardines may also be included. It is eaten with bread, not forks.

Mojo colorado ✪✪✪

A cold emulsion of paprika and cumin with chilli, oil and vinegar. Served with hot fish in the Canary Isles. The green *mojo verde* uses fresh coriander leaves, which are rare in Spain.

Mollejas ✪✪

Sweetbreads. Often stewed in wine with onion and ham.

Mongetes, monjetes

Dried white beans served with BUTIFARRA.

Montañesa, a la

From Santander, where the surrounding green region is known as 'the Mountain'.

Mora

Mulberry.

Moraga de sardinas ✪✪

A 'bundle' of fresh sardines casseroled with olive oil, wine, garlic, lemon and parsley.

Morcilla ✪✪✪

A black sausage including rice or onions, pigs' blood and often oregano. The best come from Asturias and are smoked. There is also a sweet *morcilla dulce*, sliced and eaten for *tapas*.

Morcón ✪

Ham made from the shoulder or other pork offcuts, well spiced.

Morena

The pleasant white flesh of the Moray eel. It is often found in fish stews; see CALDERETA.

Moreno ✪

A small shaped almond meringue, which is twice baked.

Moros y cristianos

A dish of black beans and white rice, commemorating an old conflict between Moors and Christians.

Morro

Cheek. Usually pork. Often stewed with beans. Calves cheek is a rarity, usually braised.

Morteruelo ✪✪

A hot hash of mixed meats including game and pounded liver, or a cold terrine, spiced with cumin.

Mostachones ✪

S-shaped biscuits, often with nuts, which combine in pairs to make a 'moustache'.

Mostaza

Mustard.

Mujol, múgil

The lesser grey mullet. It is cooked like LISA, but is famous for its cured roe.

Muslos

Usually chicken legs. Also Catalan for mussel.

Musola

The smooth-hound, a good-to-eat shark; see CAZÓN.

N

Nabo

Turnips, *naps* in Catalan.

Naranja ✪

Orange. Excellent with raw onions as a starter (*ensalada de naranja*). *Naranjas acaramelizadas* is a salad, in caramel syrup. Oranges make a delicious sorbet (*sorbete*).

Nata

Cream. Uncommon in the south, and kept for desserts, like whipped cows' cream flavoured with cinnamon, sugar and lemon, or with nuts or fruit.

Natillas ✪✪

Rich custards made with many egg yolks, cinnamon and lemon zest. Excellent when very cold. Sometimes egg whites are served as accompanying meringues.

Navajas ✪
Long, brown razorshell clams. Eaten raw or steamed.

Nécoras ✪
Small shore crabs. Served boiled or in soups.

Niscalo ✪
The 'bleeding' or saffron milk cap. Spain's most pickled wild mushroom; see also ROVELLON.

Níspero ✪
Loquat. A plum-sized Easter fruit with a double seed, deep-yellow, grainy, sweet flesh and toughish skin.

Ñora
A sweet mild chilli; see ROMESCO.

Nuez
Nut. Commonly means walnut, as in *sopa de nueces* (walnut cream soup) from the walnut tree (*nogal*). *Nueces variados* are mixed unshelled nuts.

Nuez moscada
Nutmeg.

O

Oca
Young goose.

Oca con peras ✪✪
A gosling cooked with pears.

Olla
The cooking pot; see PUCHERO. *Olla gitana*, a 'gypsy pot', includes any vegetable, with fruit, such as pears. *Olleta* is another vegetable pot; in Valencia it may include game.

Olla podrida ✪✪
Literally means 'rotten pot', because the meat is simmered so long it has the softness of overripe fruit.

Orégano
Oregano.

Orejas
Pigs' ears. Often salted and popular eaten with beans.

Orejones
Dried apricots. Strung up in a ring, hence the name 'ears'.

Orelletes ✪
'Little ears' of twisted *anís* flavoured pastry, deep-fried, served with sugar or honey.

Oropesa ✪
A hard, ewes' milk, Castilian cheese, stored in olive oil.

Ortiga
Stinging nettle.

Ostra ✪✪✪
The true oyster. *Ostión* is the cheaper, cultivated so-called Portuguese oyster, a speciality found mostly round Cádiz. It is excellent coated and fried (*fritas*) in a *tartera*, with garlic and breadcrumbs, or in SOPA DEL CUARTO DE HORA.

Ous
Catalan for egg.

P

Pa amb tomàquet ✪✪✪
Served at most Catalan meals, this is toast with tomato juice squeezed over. Olive oil finishes it off and sometimes SERRANO and cheese are put on top.

Pa d'ous
Catalan for FLAN (custard dessert).

Paella a la valenciana ✪✪✪
The original *paella*, of saffron rice, with a mixture of chicken or rabbit, fish, prawns and shellfish, with peppers. There are many versions and the shellfish *paella de maiscos* is also popular in Valencia. *A la catalana* includes sausage, pork and peppers.

Paella al estilo de Parellada ✪✪
Named after Juli Parellada, a 19th-century dandy, who asked for his *paella* 'without bones or shells' in.

Home-grown Spanish oranges

Pagès
'From the countryside'. *Pan de pagès* is very solid bread.

Paire
Long thin scabbard fish. Cut diagonally and grilled.

Pajaritos
Small birds. Eaten less now that people are better off.

Paletillo
Shoulder. Used for old-fashioned dishes, like stewed mutton (*de carnero*).

Palitos
A skewer and anything on it, usually a *tapa*.

Palmeras de hojaldre ✪
A delicious biscuit consisting of two whirls of puff-pastry cut side up – the French *palmiers*.

Palmito, ensalada de
Palm heart salad. Usually with pink mayonnaise and lettuce. Fresh *palmetto* is an Easter dish.

Paloma
Dove or pigeon, *torcaz* if wild; see PICHÓN.

Palometa ✪✪
A deep-water fish, *palometa negra* is pomfret (Ray's bream), excellent to eat. The flesh is faintly pink and flakes in long strands like skate. It is good fried and worthy of rich sauces. *Palometa blanco* is pompano.

Palomitas
Popcorn.

Pan
White bread, excellent quality in Spain. Catalunya has a three-cornered loaf – which the Surrealist artist Salvador Dali stuck all over the outside of his house! Wholemeal bread is *pan integral*. *Pan rallado* is breadcrumbs.

Pan de centeno
Rye bread, made in Galicia.

Pan de higos ✪✪
Sweetmeat of dried figs, in a flat cake like the Italian *panforte*. It is coated underneath with chocolate.

Pan de pernil
Jellied ham.

Panadés ✪✪
Lamb pies in Mallorca, made at Easter,

Panadons
Catalan word for pasties. They may have spinach or fish-like tuna in them.

Panceta
Pork belly with some lean – unlike TOCINO.

Panecicos
Sweet puff made of breadcrumbs with egg white, fried then soaked in syrup.

Panecillos
Bread rolls.

Panellets ✪✪
Small sweet cakes. Made of almond paste, but sometimes sweet potato, and topped with pine nuts or almonds. They are made for All Saints' Day in many flavours.

Panquemado ✪
'Burnt bread',. a sugar-glazed breakfast bread.

Papas arrugadas ✪✪
'Wrinkled potatoes' are new potatoes boiled in seawater until salt-crusted, then baked and served with a spicy MOJO sauce. *Papas* is 'potato' in the Canary Islands.

Pargo ✪
Sea bream with rosy tints to its side and tail. Excellent as steaks, or stuffed or baked.

Parrilla, a la
From the grill.

Parrillada de pescado ✪✪✪
A mixed grill of fish. In Catalunya this may include shellfish too. (*Parrillada* following a noun is a *gratín*)

Pasas
Dried fruit, usually raisins; famous when from Málaga. *Pasas de corinto* are currants, while CIRUELAS PASAS are prunes.

Pasiego, queso de ✪
A fresh soft cheese, made into cheesecake in Santander; used to make QUESADA.

Pastas
Pasta dishes.

Pasta quebrada
Flaky pastry.

Pastel
Embraces even more food than the American term 'pie'. In most of Spain it is the word for a pastry-topped pie. *Pastel de conejo* is rabbit pie and *pastel de pescado* fish pie. Also the common word for cake, and any solid, cooked pudding.

Pastel de berenjenas
An aubergine terrine or timbale.

Pastel de hígado
Liver pâté.

Pastel de pasas
A rather soggy breadcrumb and raisin pudding. The similar *pastel de Pascua* (Easter pudding) in Mallorca is made with eggs and biscuit crumbs.

Pasteles de carne ✪
Pasties enclosing savoury meat, perhaps with chopped egg (to absorb juice) and vegetables. *Pastel murciano* is a spicy version. They are also potato cakes including chopped sausage.

Pastelvasco
See GATAVASK.

Pa amb tomàquet, *a do-it-yourself snack (see page 54)*

Pastillas
Pastilles (sweets). The milk-and-coffee caramels of Logroño are well known.

Pata
Foot. *Patas de cerdo a la parrilla* are grilled trotters.

Patacó, patacu ✪
A casserole of tuna with potato, sometimes containing snails. It can be adapted to pork.

Patatas
Potato. Diced potatoes are 'hazelnutted' (*avellanada*).

Patatas a la riojana ✪
Potatoes flavoured (and coloured) with CHORIZO.

Patatas bravas ✪✪
A popular *tapa* of potatoes in a spicy tomato sauce – very spicy in Barcelona.

Patatas castellanas ✪
Potatoes fried with plenty of paprika.

Patatas pobres
'Poor man's potatoes', with garlic and parsley.

Patatas viudas
'Widow's potatoes' with only fried onion.

Pâté en lata
Canned pâté.

RUSTIC PARTRIDGE

Partridge is a familiar dish for country folk all over Spain. Usually pot-roasted with a little wine, it is also good *amb rovellon* (with wild mushrooms).

✪✪✪ **Escabeche de perdices**
Partridges cooked in wine and a lot of vinegar, then chilled until the liquid jellies. Rabbit, *conejo en escabeche*, is also good.

✪✪✪ **Perdices a la torero** Bull-fighters are well fed and these partridges are braised with ham, tomatoes, wine and anchovies.

✪✪✪ **Perdices al chocolate** Partridges with chocolate. Found all over Spain; not sweet at all, but with a rich, dark gravy.

✪✪ **Perdices con coles** Partridges rolled in cabbage leaves.

Pato
Duck. Commonly roast, it is served in the north with turnips (*con nabos*) and in Catalunya with figs, *pato con higos*.

Pato a la sevillana ✪✪
The original 'duck with orange' from Seville, it does not taste of orange. The acidity of the bitter fruit, plus olives, cuts the fat of the pot-roast bird. *Pato con aceitunas* (duck with olives) is very similar.

Pavías de pescado
Fish fingers; see SOLDADITOS DE PAVÍA.

Pavo
Turkey. They are smaller in Spain and you may find breasts or roast birds stuffed with apples or chestnuts.

Pavo solo
Cold cooked turkey breast.

Pebre, en, all-i-pebre ✪✪
In 'pepper', ie paprika. This 'oil and pepper' sauce is very simple but good for eels (ANGUILAS), fish and chicken.

Pecho de cerdo
Belly of pork.

Pechuga de pollo ✪
Chicken breast. These may be stuffed (*rellena*), crumbed (*empanada*) and are excellent with orange sauce (*en salsa de naranja*).

Pelotas, pilotas ✪
Small meatballs, poached in broth like dumplings.

Pencas
Usually the stalks of ACELGA (Swiss chard), without the leaf.

Pepino
Cucumber. Mainly used as a plain salad. *Pepinillos* are pickled gherkins.

Pepitas
Seeds for snacks: sunflower or melon seeds.

Pepitoria de gallina (or de pollo) ✪
A fricassee of hen or chicken with a distinctive Arab ground almond and garlic sauce.

Peras
Pears.

Peras al horno/al vinto tinto
Pears baked with red wine and cinnamon.

Perca
Perch.

Percebes ✪✪
A very expensive shellfish, a speciality of Galicia, usually translated as a 'goose-neck barnacle'. It looks like a miniature bear's claw with white fingernails, and tastes of the sea.

Perdices a la capellán
The 'chaplain's partridges' are not birds, but beef rolls with ham and SOBRASADO (a type of sausage) inside.

Perdiz, perdices, perdigones, perdiú
Partridge (see box above).

Perejil
Parsley. In Spain it is flat-leaved and mild. It garnishes salads and goes into a PICADA and an ALIÑO.

Pericana ✪✪
A salted cod salad that includes crumbled pieces of fried, dried red chilli, in Valencia. It is served with COCA.

Pernil
The Catalan word for SERRANO.

Perol

A deep frying pan, used for soupy rice dishes.

Perros y gatos

'Dogs and cats' – ugly fish sold under a pet name.

Perruñillas, perruñas ✪

Sweet, cinnamon 'dog biscuits'. They bake with deep cracks. *Perruñas* are richer, flavoured with lemon zest and are coated with egg white and sugar.

Pescadillo ✪✪

The small silver hake (sometimes called whiting). This fish is less flat than many others, with fillets on top of the backbone, so it is served belly down. Larger ones are deep fried in a ring, with the tail in the mouth (*se come su cola*). Smaller ones make soup; see CALDILLO.

Pescado

Fish.

Pescaíto frito ✪✪✪

Fried fish, a star *tapa* in Cádiz.

Pestiños, pistiñes ✪✪

A sweet fritter of *anís* or wine pastry, made by overlapping the opposite corners of a square. Deep-fried until they puff, they are soaked in syrup and served with sugar or honey.

Pez ángel

Angelfish shark; see ANGELOTE.

Pez espada ✪✪✪

Swordfish. The flesh is firm, almost meaty and consequently expensive; steaks are grilled, though they can be a little dry. It may be cooked like ATÚN and is good *en* AMARILLO (in a yellow sauce).

Pez limón ✪

Amberjack, the fish with a long yellow streak. It is good grilled, baked, or as fried fillets served in sauce.

Pez martillo

Hammerhead shark. Small ones make good eating.

Picada

The addition to a sauce that thickens it. In Catalunya it is made of garlic, bread and toasted nuts.

Picadillo

'Chopped small', so usually means minced meat. *Picadillos* is a hash, and includes sausage when used for stuffing.

Pescaíto frito – *mixed fried fish*

Picante
Spicy hot. GUINDILLA is the only Spanish chilli to fear.

Picatostes ✪
Fried bread fingers or buttered toast, often sugared.

Pichón
Pigeon or squab. Probably pot-roasted with a little wine.

Pichón con pasas y piñones ✪✪✪
Pigeon with raisins and pine nuts in a sherry or sweet wine sauce.

Picón, queso de ✪✪✪
A creamy blue cheese, named for its home in the Picos de Europa; see CABRALES.

Pierna ✪✪✪
Leg, often roasted. Lamb is *de cordera*; a *la oransana* it is cooked on top of haricot beans, like the French *boulangère*. Roast kid (*pierna de cabrito*) is also delicious.

Pies
Feet; see PATA.

Pijama
The best dessert in the house: a FLAN and an ice, or two sorts of ice-cream, with three types of canned fruit is typical. It used to mean 'covered in whipped cream', and this is where the 'pyjamas' (formerly nightshirts) came in.

Pijotas
Baby hake. They are crisp-fried on the south coast.

Pilongas
Dried chestnuts. Made into a puréed soup or stewed with beans and pork.

Pil-pilando ✪✪✪
A sizzling dish; see GAMBAS PIL-PIL. One of the rare dishes served extremely hot, for

Garlic and peppers strung up to dry in the sun

Spanish food is often just warm. It has no connection with the white Basque sauce called *pil-pil*.

Pimentón
Paprika, a basic pepper in Spain.

Pimienta
Black pepper.

Pimientos
Peppers (see box below).

Piña
Pineapple.

Pinchitos morunos ✪✪
Small pork kebabs, flavoured with cumin and coriander.

Pinchos
Any food that can be skewered on a cocktail stick, almost synonomous with *tapas*.

Piñonatas
Expensive, rich-tasting little pine nut cakes.

Piñones
Pine nuts. Tiny and cream-coloured, they are extracted from the cones of stone pines, and are consequently expensive. The flavour is astringent, yet rich, much liked for sauces, vegetable dishes and cakes.

Pintada
Guinea fowl. Mainly served roasted in smart restaurants.

Pintarroja
A dogfish or small shark. Good to eat; see CAZÓN.

Pipas
Seeds. White sunflower seeds (*de girasol*) are a common snack, but pumkin (*pipas de calabaza*) and melon seeds are also sold, often in mixed packets with salted peanuts and sweetcorn.

Piperita
Peppermint.

PEPPERS – SWEET OR SPICY

Peppers (pimientos) appear in many local dishes, but are also eaten on their own stuffed with lots of interesting ingredients.

✪✪✪ **Pimientos de piquillo rellenos de bacalao** A Basque speciality of spicy, long red peppers, stuffed with salted cod, then fried and served in a sauce.

✪✪ **Pimientos fritos** Small deep-fried green peppers. Popular all over Spain, the best are from Padrón.

✪✪ **Pimientos rellenos** Stuffed peppers. Usually the familiar fat ones, with ham or pork.

✪✪✪ **Pimientos rojos asados** Roast, skinned red peppers, served as a salad with oil; very Spanish!

Piperrada ✪✪✪
A soft, creamy omlette in the French style, flavoured with puréed roast red pepper, onions and tomatoes. *Piperra* is the Basque word for 'pepper', and dishes containing them.

Pipirrana ✪✪
A salad of chopped peppers, tomato, cucumber and onion. Served very cold, this is close to GAZPACHO. It may contain BACALAO or tuna, with a dressing based on hard egg yolks; in Jaén it is served with SERRANO.

Piriñaca ✪✪
A salad of mixed chopped vegetables without cucumber. The same mixture accompanies baked fish, such as *besugo asado con piriñaca.*

Pisto ✪✪✪
A tomato, aubergine and mixed vegetable sauce, meaning a 'hotchpotch'. *Pisto manchego* includes scrambled

Pinchos, *anything on a cocktail stick (see page 61)*

egg. Good with fish too (*pisto de peces*).

Pixin
Monkfish; see RAPE.

Plancha, a la
On the hot iron (griddle): a way of grilling with very little oil.

Plátanos
Bananas.

Plátanos fritos ✪✪✪
Fried bananas. Popular in the Canary Islands.

Platija
Flounder (fish); the name means 'flat'. Good to eat.

Platos fríos
Cold dishes.

Pochas
Haricot beans. Eaten fresh.

Pochas con codornices ✪✪✪
Fresh haricots cooked with quail. The dish opens the hunting season.

Pochas riojanas ✪✪
Fresh haricots cooked with CHORIZO, which reddens the podded beans.

Poleo
Type of mint.

SPANISH CHEESE

Spanish cheese is either hard or very fresh; compared with France, Spain lacks the whole middle range of matured creamy cheeses. However, there are many unusual hand-made cheeses, mainly using unpasteurised milk. There are a few semi-hard cheeses, like CANTABRIA, but it is the hard cheeses that mature to distinction. Most Spanish hard cheeses pass from mild when semi-hard, to strong and sharp when hard. Some hard cheese is stored in olive oil, which allows it to mature without drying out: attractive examples are from Oropesa and those exported from Burgos by Gúzman. Creamy blue cheeses are made, much in the same style as Roquefort, like *cabarales.*

Hard and soft cheeses bear the marks of rope moulds. The wrapping (like a Dick Whittington bundle) shows up on the Levantine *servilleta*, while PUZOL has a conical depression in the middle. Soft cottage and fresh cheeses are made all over the country. Spain has no long tradition of cooking with cheese – it is mostly eaten with bread before or after a meal. However, the hard cheeses grate well.

Pollastre amb gambes ✪✪✪
Catalan chicken with prawns, in a red wine and pine nut sauce.

Pollo
Chicken. *Rebozado* is coated with breadcrumbs and fried. *Al jerez* is finished with sherry and *a la granadina* also includes raw ham. *Pollo con aceitunas* is stewed gently with green olives. *Pollo en arroz* (chicken in rice) is common on the north coast; see CAMPURRIANO.

Pollo al chilindrón ✪✪
Chicken cooked with peppers, tomatoes and onions. *Pollo en chanfaina* is similar; see SAMFAINA.

Pollo asado ✪✪
Spanish chickens are often roasted with pork fat, salt and paprika, which makes their skin wonderfully tasty. Also good roasted *con salsa de naranja* (basted with orange juice).

Polvorones ✪✪✪
'Crumble cakes'. As this is what these little cakes do very easily, they are paper-wrapped. The best ones include ground almonds as well as flour and sugar, flavoured with *anís* and cinnamon. They are made all over Spain, but those from Antequera are outstanding. Accompany them with a glass of *anís* or OLOROSO sherry.

Pomelo
Grapefruit.

Porchella asado ✪✪✪
Roast suckling pig in Mallorca.

Porra antequerana ✪✪
A very thick type of GAZPACHO with raw ham.

Postre
Like the English 'afters', it means dessert.

Postre de músico
A Christmas dish of nuts and dried fruits.

Potaje ✪
A thick vegetable soup – pottage. *Potaje de valenciana* has chick-peas and spinach, *potaje murciana* has rice, green beans and FRIJOLES (dried beans).

Pote asturiana ✪✪
A thick soup of beans and sausage. *Pote primavera* is a mix of spring vegetables. *Pote granadina* contains tomato, peppers and onions, probably with saffron.

Poti poti ✪
Salted cod salad, with potatoes and peppers.

Pringadas
Fried bread, often with bacon or sausage. The name comes from a verb that means 'to fry in bacon fat'.

Puchero
An earthenware cooking pot, and so a stew. The Andalucían *puchero* usually contains a range of vegetables and even tomato sauce, while in the Canary Isles *puchero canario* has pumpkin, sweetcorn, sweet potato, even pears.

Pudín
Like English pudding, it can take lots of forms, including anything moulded. It can mean a cold meat or fish mould or even a hot meat loaf! In Mallorca, it is a cold egg and bread pudding.

Puerro
Leek.

Manchego, *Spain's best known cheese*

Pulpeta
A slice of meat; it may be rolled with a filling.

Pulpo
Octopus. Pulpitas are baby ones and likely to be more tender.

Pulpo a la feria   ✪✪✪
A famous Galician dish of boiled octopus served in a paprika-oil salad dressing. This is usually a salad, but might come hot from the pot.

Puntillitas
Small squid. Fried in batter as a *tapa*.

Purrusalda, porrosaldo   ✪✪
A Basque leek and potato soup. This usually includes cooked BACALAO.

Puzol, queso de   ✪
A fresh cows' milk cheese in Valencia, moulded with a conical indent.

Q

Quemada
'Burnt', meeaning topped with caramelised sugar. Sweet bread and ice-cream prepared this way are both good.

Quesada, quesadilla
Cheesecake.

Queso
Cheese (see panel page 63).

Queso frito   ✪✪
Fried cheese. Slices are egged and bread-crumbed then fried.

Quisquilla
The common prawn.

R

Raba   ✪✪
A north coast squid dish, breadcoated, then fried.

Rábano
Red radish. *Rábano picante* is the stronger horseradish.

Rabo de toro estofado   ✪✪✪
Bull's tail, slow-stewed with onions and tomatoes, or with sherry (*a la jerezana*).

Rana, ancas de
Frogs' legs. Fried with garlic and parsley.

Rancho canario ✪
A stew in the Canary Isles with dried beans, potatoes and pasta, plus a little CHORIZO and bacon.

Rape ✪
Monkfish. Hugely popular in Spain. It is fried with paprika (*en pimentón*) in the south. *Al estilo de Costa Brava*, it is stewed with tomatoes, red peppers, white wine and fresh peas. Cold, it makes an excellent salad (*ensalada*).

Rascacio
Rascasse (fish). It is a favourite for fish soups and stocks, but can be cooked like DENTÓN.

Raspas de anchoas ✪✪
Anchovy backbones, deep-fried for a *tapa*. It sounds terrible, but is actually crunchy and tasty.

Raya
The wingflaps of skates (the ray shark). Good to eat, for the flesh falls from the bones in attractive strips: especially good with something acid like capers or lemon juice. Skate is marinated then served *en adobo* in the south.

Raya en pimentón ✪
Skate wings cooked with paprika.

Rebanada
Slice, eg of bread. *Rebañar* means 'to wipe round the plate' – it is good manners here not to leave food on the plate.

Rebeco
Chamoix.

Rebozado
Battered – 'hidden in a shawl' – and deep fried.

Recuit ✪
A soft fresh cheese, eaten with honey or sugar.

Redondo
Part of the beef rump, tied and roasted in a joint.

Rellena
Stuffed. From peppers (usually the slim, hot ones) to red cabbage to pig's trotters; fillings are often meat and sausage.

Remojón ✪
A BACALAO salad, the name means 'soaked', for this is how the fish is prepared. There are several versions: one with oranges, another with peppers, potatoes, olives and hard-boiled eggs.

Rémol
Brill (fish). It is cooked like RODABALLO.

Remolacha
Beetroot.

Reo
Sea trout, formerly called salmon trout because of its pink flesh. Cooked like SALMÓN.

Repaplos
A version of bread and milk, little balls of egg and crumbs are fried, then served in milk and cinnamon.

Repollo
Drumhead cabbage.

Requesón ✪
Smooth cottage cheese, often bearing pretty mould marks. In Madrid, cheeses from Miraflores and El Paular are traditional.

Revuelto con ajetes ✪✪✪
Scrambled eggs with green garlic shoots.

Revueltos con espárragos trigueros ✪✪✪
Scrambled eggs with wild asparagus: a springtime speciality.

Revuelto de setas ✪✪✪
Scrambled eggs with wild mushrooms.

Revueltos
Stirred (scrambled) eggs. Unlike TORTILLA, which is a dense egg cake.

Riñonada
Kidneys in their fat, so roasted, or a kidney and other offal mix.

Riñones al jerez ✪✪✪
Kidneys in sherry sauce. In poorer areas, this is made with pigs' kidneys and ham in tomato sauce. An excellent dish with veal or lambs' kidneys, and a universal *tapa*.

Rioja, a la
Rioja style. Good red peppers grow in Rioja and paprika is also made. Probably a dish *a la Rioja* will contain them, or red CHORIZO sausage, which include the paprika.

Robioles ✪
A small fried Easter pastry that contains custard or CABELLO DE ÁNGEL jam.

Rodaballo
Turbot. An expensive fish.

Rodabello al albariño ✪✪✪
Turbot fillets poached in white wine sauce.

Rollitos
Little rolls, containing cheese, ham, meat or

Serrano ham for sale in the delicatessen

fish. Or sweet ones, like *rollitos de aquor-diente* and *rollets*.

Rollo de carne
Meat loaf.

Romana, a la ✪✪
Any fish or shellfish battered then deep-fried. Generously, Italy is credited for something done superlatively well in Spain.

Romero
Rosemary.

Romesco de pescado ✪✪✪
A fish or shellfish dish on the east coast, sometimes containing dried beans, to which ROMESCO sauce is added before serving.

Romesco, salsa ✪✪✪
An exceptional sauce, made of ground toasted almonds and hazlenuts, with the special sweet, mild chilli called *romesco* in the Catalan country. It is excellent with fried fish or roast chicken.

Roncal, queso de ✪
A mild, medium-hard ewes' milk cheese, shaped like a small drum. It develops holes the size of rice. Factory-made in Navarra, it is well regarded, most of it going to France.

Rosada
The Spanish equivalent of 'rockfish', a name for anonymous varieties of dogfish (shark) and a saltwater catfish. Always sold skinned,

they are very pink-fleshed. Many are good to eat, but need an acid marinade.

Roscón de Reyes ✪✪
A big Twelfth-Night ring yeast cake, scented with orange-flower water. The flavour and coarse texture are much like the Italian *panettone*. The crust is sprinkled with chopped nuts and fruit, and traditionally it has a single charm hidden in it.

Roscos ✪
Doughnuts. Frequently flavoured with aniseed, they are made into rings and deep-fried. The most delicious ones are made in Burgos. *Rosquillas* are ring-shaped doughnuts or buns, made of batter, rich scone or even puff pastry, and ususally a generous amount of egg. They are fried or baked, then glazed.

Rosquillas de Alcalá ✪
Pastry rings, frosted twice, first with egg then sugar syrup.

Rosquillas de Santa Clara ✪
Rings dipped in a meringue made with syrup and rebaked.

Rosquillas tontas y listas ✪
'Rich or poor' buns, some iced with sugar, others plain.

Rossejat
An oven rice dish, which often uses leftovers from COCIDO MADRILEÑO. It is 'browned' by brushing the top with egg.

Rovellon ✪✪
Spain's favourite wild mushroom. It grows in pinewoods on mountains all over the country. Bright saffron colour, it belongs to the milkcap family, but the drops it sheds when cut are red like blood. It is usually fried with parsley and garlic, and is always expensive.

Rubio
The red gurnard. Good grilled and better baked with a sauce as it can be dry.

S

Sábalo
Shad, a freshwater fish. Often served as ESCABECHE as it deteriorates fast once caught. It is also fried and served in a variety of sauces.

Sal
Salt; *salado* is salted. Fish are baked whole in salt, which is broken open, then discarded at the table; see DORADA A LA SAL.

Salazón, en
Cured, that is, salted meat or fish.

Salchichas ✪✪
Fresh sausages. Excellent braised in sherry.

Salchichón ✪✪
A good, cured, ready-to-eat sausage – like salami. *Salchichón de Málaga* has whole peppercorns in it.

Salema
One of the breams (fish); see DENTÓN.

Salmón
Salmon. They are caught in the north of the country. Steaks (*toros*) are grilled, while *arroz con salmón* is a good rice dish.

Salmón a la gallega ✪✪
Galician salmon. Cooked in stock and AGUARDIENTE, then served cold.

Salmón a la ribereña ✪✪
'River' salmon steaks, fried

with raw ham, then served in a simple cider sauce.

Salmón ahumado
Smoked salmon.

Salmonete ✪✪
'Little salmon' are red mullet. Splendid grilled whole *a la parrilla*. Tiny ones are fried and have the most beautiful flavour.

Salmorejo ✪✪
From 'cold set', this has become a word for game terrines; for example *perdices en salmorejo* are potted partridges.

Salmorejo cordobés ✪✪✪
Wonderful version of chilled GAZPACHO. A cream of garlic bread, tomatoes and oil, beaten to a light emulsion, with ham and chopped hard-boiled eggs. But beware! Sometimes it consists of just garlic, vinegar, oil and puréed bread.

Salmuera, en
In brine.

Salones
Literally 'salted', this may be cured lamb, kid or beef. The *salazones* of Valencia are salted, wind-dried fish, such as BONITO.

Salpicón de mariscos ✪✪
A shellfish 'cocktail' or salad; the French term means 'chopped' ingredients bound together in a sauce. It can also be made with chicken (*de pollo*).

Salsa
Sauce. *Salsa de tomate* includes ketchup as well as tomatoes.

Salteado
Sautéed.

Salvia
Sage.

Sama de pluma
A bream (fish); see DENTÓN.

Samfaina ✪✪✪
One of the great Catalan sauces, and also a vegetable dish in its own right. It is made from aubergines, courgettes and peppers in an onion and tomato sauce. Chicken, pork and BACALAO are all cooked in it.

San Jacobo ✪✪
An international steak: Beef fillet covered with ham and cheese.

San Pedro ✪
St Peter's fish has a black finger-print on either side of its big head and is extremely tasty, with four big, bone-

free fillets, It is also called *pez John Dory* and cooked in the same way as LUBINA.

San Simón, queso de ✪✪
A famous cows' milk cheese in Galicia, now factory made. It is smoked and looks like a well-oiled brown pear.

Sancocho canario ✪✪✪
A fish stew, best made of DENTÓN with potatoes. In the Canary Isles, it is served with a powerful red sauce that includes chillies and vinegar.

Sandía
Watermelon.

Santiaguiño ✪
The flat clawless Galician lobster. It has the cross of St James on its head, hence the name. It is also called a *cigarra de mar* (sea cricket) because it clicks in the water.

Sardinas ✪✪
Sardines. These are lovely barbecued simply on the beach. *A la santanderina* they are casseroled in tomato sauce.

Sargo
A bream. Good grilled or baked; see DENTÓN.

Sartén, de
'From the frying pan', as in *dulce de sartén* (deep-fried sweet pastries).

Seco
Dry or dried.

Sepia
Cuttlefish. Like purse-shaped squid; their flesh is sweeter but tougher. Small ones are grilled, but they are usually chopped and braised. The black ink from inside – the

Typical ingredients for an Andalucian snack

original sepia ink – is used to finish the sauce.

Sepia con guisantes ✪✪
A pleasant stew of cuttlefish with peas.

Sequillos ✪
Hazlenut meringues.

Serrano, jamón ✪✪✪
The name means 'mountain-ham', usually called simply *serrano*. Eaten thinly sliced and raw on bread, as a *tapa*, or chopped for cooking. The best ham is *pata negra*, from black pigs running wild, and recognisable by the black toes of the trotter. The king of hams comes from Jabugo, north of Huelva. Others are made at Trevélez (less salty) and Montánchez. Less expensive (and leaner) hams are made from the white pig, and also from the shoulder (so not strictly ham). An amazing number of dishes include ham or ham stock.

Sesos
Brains. These are often included with other meats. *Sesos huecos* – nicknamed 'scatter-brains' – are creamy light fritters.

Setas ✪✪✪
A general term for all wild mushrooms. They are ususally fried simply with garlic and parsley, occasionally with ham. They are also often served with eggs and as part of a game dish.

Setas a la llauna ✪✪
Wild mushrooms baked 'in a metal dish' in the oven with pork fat and garlic, in Catalunya.

Sidra, a la
Cooked in cider. Many fish are cooked this way on the north coast, often with potatoes, which are fried first, then soaked in the sauce.

Sobrasada ✪✪
A soft, raw, red pork sausage, flavoured with paprika and with a great deal of fat. It is often served in pots, without the sausage casing, and is popular in Mallorca.

Sofrito
Onions fried slowly with garlic and parsley. This is a basic of Spanish cooking; tomato is added to make a sauce. The adjective means 'lightly fried'.

Soldaditos de Pavía ✪✪
The original fish finger. The Spanish equiv-alent of bread-and-butter 'soldiers', they are fried hake or BACALAO and commemorate the 'soldiers of General Pavía', who overthrew the first republic in 1874.

Solla
Not sole but plaice. Cooked like LENGUADO.

Solomillo
Beef fillet steak, from inside the sirloin bone. It may be roasted whole and served with fried onion rings.

Solomillo andaluz
Pork tenderloin – an economy version of beef fillet. *A la Trianera* (named after the Cádiz gypsy quarter) – roasted in sherry.

Sopa
Soup, made of the basic vegetables like *cebolla* (onion) as well as with rice (*sopa de arroz*) and pasta (*de fideos*). *Venduras* usually includes dried beans.

Sopa AB or de vino ✪✪
Named after the *amontillado* sherry from Gonzales Byass used in it.

Sopa aragonesa ✪✪
Made of minced calf's liver, grated cheese and broth, it is finished with a crust of bread and cheese.

Sopa castellana ✪✪
Garlic soup with cumin from La Mancha.

Sopa de ajo ✪✪✪
Basically this is water thickened with bread and flavoured with garlic: it can be appalling, but has many admirers. In Avila the bread for the *sopa de pobre* (for 'the poor') is fried first. In Rioja or Castile, it may have eggs beaten into it, and paprika for colour, Elsewhere it may contain poached eggs. The *sopa de gato*, cat soup in Cádiz, has grated cheese, and in Aragón garlic soup has lots of lemon.

Sopa de albóndigas ✪✪
Chicken broth with veal and ham meatballs, flavoured with cinnamon.

Sopa de almendras ✪✪
A sweet of almonds and bread, flavoured with cinnamon and lemon zest.

Sopa de cangrejos ✪✪
Delicious crab bisque, made in Mallorca.

Sopa de mariscos or ✪✪✪
de pescados
Shellfish soup and fish soup. Often inter-changeable: both contain both. Sometimes one fish is singled out, as in *sopa de gambas*

(prawn soup); *sopa de pescadilla* (silver hake) or *sopa de rape* (monkfish). If you can afford it, *sopa de langosta* is lobster (crawfish) soup.

Sopa de mejillones ✪✪
Mussel soup. Good in Catalunya, with tomato, garlic and AGUARDIENTE.

Sopa de picadillo ✪✪
The name means soup with a 'chopped garnish' of ham, hard boiled eggs and fresh mint – the latter as a hangover cure. There are many egg and ham soups, like *sopa alpurrañas.*

Sopa de tomate ✪✪
A soup with a long history in Cádiz, made with tomatoes and red peppers.

Sopa del cuarto de hora ✪✪
This '15-minute' soup – quick compared to a broth – contains fried onions and rice. It may have prawns and chopped ham and hard-boiled eggs in it. In Cádiz, it may contain Portuguese oysters.

Sopa mahimones, maimones ✪✪
An Arab garlic, bread and olive oil soup, possibly with ham. It is finished in the oven to poach the eggs in it. Very hot and strong, it is especially good when you are tired and broke!

Sopa mallorquina ✪
Contains tomatoes, onions and peppers, but is made very solid, with bread and not much liquid.

Sopas cachorreñas ✪✪
A fish soup flavoured with pounded bitter orange zest, vinegar and oil.

Soplillos
Fried sweet puffs with *anís* or meringues with toasted almonds.

Sospiros de Moros
Big puffy dry meringues in Granada.

Suflé
A soufflé. Usually less good in Spain than in France.

Suizos, bollos
Breakfast rolls, slashed down the middle and baked with sugar or currants in the hollow. The name means 'Swiss' – how different from Swiss roll!

Suquet, susquet, ✪✪✪
susquillo de pescador
A Catalan soup-stew with many sorts of fish and shellfish, laced with brandy and based on onions and tomatoes, probably with

potatoes. Some are thickened with pounded almonds.

Suspiros de monja
'Nun's sighs', a popular dessert of soft meringues poached in milk then served with custard. Known as *oeufs à la neige* in Britain and France and 'floating islands' in the United States. *Suspiros* are usually dry meringues.

T

Tapa, tapaplana ✪✪
Beef; lower rump

Tarrina, en
Little brown eartherware pots are used for CUAJADA and soft cheese – the Spanish equivalent of French white ramekins.

Tarta
Usually a cake or sweet pastry. *Tartita* is any small dessert, including ice-cream in pots.

Tarta de almendras ✪
Almond cake, often just ground almonds. egg yolks and sugar, like that from Puentedueme in Galicia.

Tarta de manzana
Apple tart, often of puff pastry.

Tarta de Santiago ✪✪
In Santiago de Compostela on St James's Day, this is a pastry tart enclosing a moist almond filling. The topping is decorated with a stencil of St James's sword. In Madrid, however, they dispense with the pastry and consequently it is a rather drier ground almond cake.

Tarta helada
An ice-cream layer cake. *Tarta al whisky* has two different vanilla ice-creams, a whisky sponge layer and caramelised sugar on top.

Tarta Pasiega
A cheesecake, of fresh cheese of the type made in the Basque region, often flavoured with *anís*.

Tejas ✪
'Tiles'. Thin biscuits of egg white, ground almonds and sugar, like the French *tuiles*.

Tenca
Tench, a freshwater fish. Good marinated then fried or as ESCABECHE.

Ternasco asado ✪✪✪
Baby lamb, roasted with white wine and lemon, a speciality in Aragón and Navarra.

Ternera
Often translated as 'veal', this is nearer to being virgin beef, as it can be up to two years old. *Ternera mechada* is 'larded', for a pot-roast or roast – good with *castañas* (chestnuts).

Ternera a la sevillana ✪✪
Veal cooked in Montilla wine, with olives.

Ternera con alcachofas ✪✪
Veal escalopes and artichoke bases in a sherry or tomato sauce.

Terrina
Cold terrrine or pâté.

Tetilla, queso de ✪
A breast-shaped, soft white cow's milk cheese, now factory-made in Galicia.

Tirabeques
Mangetout peas.

Tocino
Pork fat, fresh or salted, cut from the belly, and almost solid fat, even though it is the same cut as streaky bacon. It is cubed and fried to make a fine-flavoured fat for cooking (and crisp bits) used in bean dishes. Sometimes *tocino* is fried bacon.

Tocino de cielo ✪✪✪
A dessert of pure sweetness and wonderful texture, it is served in small squares. Made from syrup and egg yolks, the name means 'heavenly bacon', because it looks like a slab of bacon, as the sugar caramelises on top.

Tojunto
'All together'; *todo junto* is a one-pot mix of vegetables, rabbit and meat.

Tomates rellenos ✪✪
Stuffed tomatoes. In Alicante, spinach, nuts and orange are used.

Tomillo, en
With thyme, a popular herb.

Torradas
Fried TORRIJA, incorporated into a sweet omelette or custard.

Torrados
Toasted chick-peas.

Torreznos
Crisp, thick strips of fried pork belly.

Torrija ✪
A children's dessert of bread dipped in milk then fried and sugared. Like French *pain perdu*, it is made to use up stale bread.

Torta
A flat bun or a round or oval breakfast bread topped with crunchy sugar. It can also be a tart or a cake.

Torta de aceite
Plain pastry biscuits, made with oil.

Torta del Casar ✪✪
You are in luck if you find this rich, aromatic, Extremeño ewes' milk cheese.

Tortas de hojaldre
Cake consisting of puff pastry layers with jam.

TRUE SPANISH OMELETTE

A round golden egg and potato cake, about the thickness of a sponge layer, this is *the* Spanish omelette. Delicious when well made, it is eaten hot, warm or cold, and is popular as a picnic filling in rolls. Wedges are speared on sticks as *tapas*.

There are many variations on the classic *tortilla española*, for example *espinacas* is with spinach and *gambas* is with prawns. *Tortilla hormigas o formigos* 'with ants' has crispy MIGAS (fried breadcrumbs) in it. A plain omelette is a *tortilla francesa*.

✪✪ **Tortilla a la catalana** is an omelette with beans and BUTIFARRA sausage.

✪✪ **Tortilla de Tudela** or **espárragos** is asparagus omelette.

✪✪ **Tortilla gallega** is an omelette with CHORIZO sausage and peppers.

✪ **Tortilla guisada** is served in tomato sauce.

✪ **Tortilla murciana** contains tomato and red peppers.

✪✪ **Tortilla paisana** often has a mixture of CHORIZO, potatoes, peppers, tomatoes, the lot!

✪✪✪ **Tortilla Sacramonte** is a famous (or infamous) gypsy omelette from Granada, with soft, smooth, white lambs' brains and (nowadays) sweetbreads, crisp MIGAS, peppers and potatoes.

Tortells
A breakfast bread ring with a ground almond and lemon filling – and potato too – though you can't taste it.

Tortilla española ✪✪✪
Spanish omelette. *Truita* is Catalan for tortilla. (See box page 71).

Tortillitas de berenjenas ✪✪
Aubergine fritters.

Tostadas
Literally 'toast'. Bread only very lightly grilled to freshen it, and used to mop up sauces. Alternatively it can be fried.

Tostadas de crema ✪
Not toast, but breakfast fingers of cold custard, egged and breadcrumbed, then fried.

Tostón ✪✪✪
Roast suckling pig.

Toyina
Salted tuna.

Trigo
Whole wheat, soaked. A *guiso de trigo* or *triguillo* is a soup with turnips and ACELGA stalks or squash. *Olla de trigo* contains chickpeas flavoured with CHORIZO, bacon and chilli.

Trixat
Spanish bubble and squeak. Cooked potato and cabbage, plus chopped bacon, are pressed into a mould then fried as a cake in pork fat.

Truchas
Trout. Brown trout still swim in the fast streams of the Pyrenees and Asturias, though restaurant ones are likely to be farmed and pink. Usually fried but good ESCABECHE.

Truchas a la montañesa ✪✪
Cantabrican trout cooked with white wine, onion and bay leaves. There is also a red wine version (*en vino tinto*) in Navarra.

Truchas almendras ✪✪
Trout fried and served with fried almonds, or *con salsa de almendras*, usually a ground almond sauce.

Truchas con jamón ✪✪✪
Ham slices are fried, then trout are fried in the ham fat and served stuffed or wrapped in ham. This is called *truchas a la navarra*.

A real Spanish omelette – colourful, rich and satisfying

Trufa
Truffle. Found all over Spain but chiefly near Castellón de la Plana on the east coast.

Trumfes fadrines
Potatoes on their own, served with a little ham and egg-thickened sauce added at the last minute.

Ttoro, tioro ✪
A Basque mixed fish stew or soup, with onion, bread and wine.

Tuétano
Bone marrow. Ususally grilled slices.

Tumbet, tombet ✪
A vegetable stew from Mallorca, with tomatoes and aubergine, like *ratatouille* with potatoes added. Sometimes it is layered with meat or contains eggs, and there are also fish versions.

Turrón ✪✪✪
A candy-like Italian *nougat*. *Jijona blando* is a soft coffee-coloured paste of ground toasted almonds and honey. Alicante *turrón* is white and hard, studded with whole nuts.

Txangurro, changurro
The Basque word for a spider crab; see CENTOLLO.

U

Urta a la roteña ✪✪✪
A bream, related to DENTÓN. Found on the southwest coast, it feeds on shellfish and so tastes of them. It is cooked in a naturally-sweet sauce made by frying onions until they caramelise, then adding tomato which is reduced very slowly.

Uvas blancas (negras)
White (black) grapes.

V

Vaca
Cow, giving beef and milk for *queso de vaca*, cheese.

Venado
Venison. A coarse meat, it is often stewed with thyme.

Venado con cabrales ✪✪✪
The best cuts of venison roasted and with a blue cheese sauce.

Veneras
Scallops.
Verduras
Green
vegetables.
Often a
separate course,
or included in rice or
MENESTRA.
Vieiras
The Galician name for scallops.
Vieiras al alberiño ✪✪
Scallops cooked in the local white wine.
**Vieiras de Santiago or
Santiagüenses** ✪✪
Scallops in Santiago de Compostela are
flamed in brandy, arranged in the upper shell
with tomato sauce and topped with bread-
crumbs, then quicky grilled.
Vieja ✪
The colourful 'widow' fish, purpled backed
and yellow finned, is very typical of the
Canary Isles. It has very delicate flesh, which
is poached with potatoes.
Villalón, queso de ✪
A soft rectangular ewes' milk cheese in
Castile, sometimes shaped like a hoof.
Villeroy ✪✪
A French dish, popular in Spain, of chicken
breasts or prawns coated in béchamel,
chilled then crumbed. They are fried and
served hot.
Vinagre
Vinegar. The best, *jerez*, is made from
sherry.
Vinagreta
Vinaigrette.
Viuda
'Widowed'. The word can apply to a
meatless POTAJE and to PATATAS – and also to
small, grey snails.
Vizcaína
The Spanish word for Biscay. *Salsa a la
vizcaina* includes onions and dried peppers,
but not tomato.

X

Xató, xatonada ✪✪
Mixed dressed salad from Tarragona
containing salted cod, sometimes tuna and
anchovy fillets, and often tomato and olives.

Xuxos
Fried doughnuts. Nowadays served
with whipped cream, originally fried
round a stick, then custard-filled.

Y

Yemas ✪✪✪
Very sweet, small yellow cakes. Named
after the egg yolks used to make them and
which they resemble. Nuns make these
candies by combining egg yolks with boiling
syrup. The egg paste is then moulded into
'yolk shapes', sugared and left to dry. *Yemas
de San Leandro* in Seville and those of *Santa
Teresa* in Avila are celebrated.
Yogur
Yoghurt.

Z

Zamorana, a la
Dishes from Zamora. These often include
black MORCILLA, onion and paprika.
Zanahoria
Carrot.
Zapata, zapatero
Means a 'shoe', but this is a fish of the
bream family; see DENTÓN.
Zarangollo ✪
A hash of onion and courgettes, well-
garlicked, and served with fried bread.
Zarzuela ✪✪✪
Given the name 'light opera' this dish is a
wonderful medley of white fish with a
display of shellfish in a tomato, wine and
saffron broth. A culinary star on the Catalan
coast.
Zizak
Basque for St George's mushroom; see
MOIXERNON.
Zoque
Chilled, strained, vinegared, raw tomato and
pepper soup, much like GAZPACHO. Served
over bread or TOSTADAS.
Zorza
Fried pork with paprika, like skinless CHORIZO.
Zurrón
Means a knapsack, or a small game bag, so
in culinary terms something stuffed, such as
small birds inside peppers.

Wine & Drink of Spain

Above: *treading the first grapes*
Right: *Simple but sustaining fare of fresh bread, wine, olives and grapes*

Wine & Drink of Spain

Vineyards cover a huge area of Spain, but even the famous ones may look scrubby and ill-kempt to those familiar with French or German vines. Spaniards have never made a fetish of matching 'appropriate' wines with food. And nowadays even the connection between regional food and regional wine hardly exists. This is because the Spanish wine industry has been ruthlessly restructured on commercial lines. The new wines, however, are of a type tourists are likely to enjoy, because they are mainly based on French models.

In the 1970s the sherry houses became involved in making red and white wine. They researched international markets and started producing wines to suit those palates. The Spanish themselves liked the new wines , which are now widely sold in Spain.

Spanish beer has more than five per cent alchohol per volume, making it stronger than most European beer. Spain is also a major producer of brandy and liqueurs. Excellent mineral waters abound, from Vichy Catalan on the Costa Brava to Lanjarón from the springs of the Alpujarra mountains south of Granada. Try the unusual refreshing soft drinks from one of the street stalls that spring up everywhere in summer; freshly made and iced fruit juices are guaranteed to satisfy the thirst.

Spanish grapes awaiting the harvest

Wine Producing Regions

When the *phylloxera* louse devastated the French vineyards in the 1860s, French wine-makers moved south. They settled in the two areas which are now famous for quality wine in Spain: Rioja and Penedès. Here they introduced French methods of viniculture and even French grapes, so bottles from these two areas contain the better wines on a wine list.

In the following text the denominated wine areas (DO) are given in bold.

RIOJA

In Spain there is the welcome opportunity to drink quality wines at a lower cost than elsewhere in Europe. In the Ebro valley in northern Spain, Rioja is celebrated for medium reds. The characteristic that distinguishes them as Spanish wines is a distinct flavour of vanilla, which comes from storage in oak casks. They have a softer, less

Vintage Rioja wine

delicate, but fruitier taste than French wines of equal quality. Rioja also makes respectable white wines.

Rioja wines are produced by a few major companies these days and they are very definitely blended wines – some firms actually own no vineyards at all! They buy grapes and mix varieties, so you are buying blending skill and a brand name.

On the one hand, there are the traditional houses that believe in maturing the wine in oak casks (see CRIANZA) until it absorbs a positive flavour of oak. Marqués de Murrieta is the most imposing of these, but others are Paternina, CUNE and Bodegas Riojanas. Some newer firms, like Muga, make quality wines the old way, too. The easiest to remember are the 'three mighty Ms'- Muga and the Marquéses of Murrieta and Riscal. The law specifies minimum periods in the barrel, but traditional houses may exceed this, and older wines are also likely to have a longer barrel age. La Rioja Alta's Viña Ardanza, for example, spends longer in the cask than in the bottle.

On the other hand, there are the modern *bodegas* that have gone for the minimum barrel ageing (see CRIANZA). They favour maturing in the bottle instead. The Marqués de Cáceres and Langunilla are in this camp, along with Olarro and Spain's third biggest exporter, Faustino Martínez (their labels have a face on them). The last two are popular in America.

Almost all white Rioja wine is made from the traditional Viura grape. White wine is also made in two different styles. The traditional way is to age it in oak, like red wine. Marqués de Murrieta is the most renowned white in this style. Try their RESERVA, which is lemony, but rich and buttery with the flavour of oak, or Monte Reál from Bodegas Riojanas or a white from López de Heredia. A new popular white is CUNE's Monopole *blanco*. This has only a modest amount of oakiness, and a freshness that is halfway to the new style. The new style whites are more like French wines and are made in vats. The results are crisper and fresher, with more fruit flavour. The best of these is Marqués de Cáceres, a 'poor man's Sancerre'.

Apart from the actual method of malting wine, geography is an important factor in taste – the wine-makers have, after all, to get their grapes from somewhere. Written at the bottom of each wine label is the headquarters of the firm.

Wines from the **Rioja Baja** (the lower southern end) are the fruitier, everyday wines. The cooler, higher end, the **Rioja Alta**, produces wines with the highest acidity. This means they are hard when young, but mature into something more complex. Rioja Alta RESERVAS are likely to be smooth, firm and of a high quality.

There is a third Rioja district called the **Rioja Alavesa**, which is made up of parcels of land or on the north side of Rioja Alta. The wines from here are softer, more aromatic and sometimes fuller-bodied.

NAVARRA AND ARAGÓN

Navarra is the district adjoining Rioja, and its wines share many characteristics with those of Rioja. Well balanced reds are made in the Ribera Alta and lighter ones in Valdizarbe.

Young Navarra reds are rather like *Beaujolais nouveau*. Chivite is the name to look for. Navarra also makes the best-finished ROSADOS in Spain: try Gran Feudo.

In **Aragón**, hefty purplish–coloured reds, often 15 per cent or more alcohol, are made in **Cariñena**; they have slightly more balancing acidity than the dull reds from the south. **Borja** reds are similar, with strong ROSADOS, but in **Somontano** the reds are lighter.

NORTHEAST COAST

The main difference between **Penedés** and Rioja is that Rioja is famed for wine aged in oak, (but Penedés choose the French style of bottle ageing instead – and introduced French grapes). Penedès is predominantly a white wine region, with good vines growing in the cooler hills. It is one of the main areas of experiment in Spain, the best wines being made from acclimatised foreign grapes, or from these mixed with Spanish grapes.

The big producer here is Torres. Their easy summer white wine Viña Sol – fresh, dry and a bit lemony – is made exclusively from Parellada, the Spanish grape, though in the French style. Torres Gran Viña Sol has a slight pineapple taste because it is made from half Chardonnay grapes, while the rich white and much grander Gran Viña Sol 'Green Label', made with some Sauvignon grapes, is unusual both in being estate-bottled (at Castell de Fransola) and as one of the few white wines matured in oak.

Far less red wine is made. Gran Sangre de Toro, deep red and fruity, is one of the few still typical of wine produced in the region in times past. Torres Gran Coronas, however, is more than half Cabernet Sauvignon, which gives it body and

A traditional wine press from Villafranca de Penedès, capital of the Penedès wine region

fruitiness, while the luscious – and expensive –'Black Label' is all Cabernet Sauvignon.

Another experimental (and tiny) firm is owned by American Jean León, who specialises in classic imported vine varieties. Raimat, in the **Costers de Segre**, is known for quality wines, one being a Cabernet Sauvignon. Raimat Abadia also includes the Cabernet Sauvignon grape. Raimat also makes a rich buttery-tasting white from another grape new to Spain, Chardonnay. There are also some luscious Chardonnay *caves.*

Firms like Masia Bach specialise in old indigenous vine varieties. This company makes one of the very few fresh but sweet Spanish white wines (see Dessert Wines, page 83). **Alella** is the second major wine area in Catalunya, and its whites are popular in Barcelona, for the district is just north of the city. Marqués de Alella makes delicate young white wines, with a prickly edge. **Tarragona** is also white wine country, and famed for dessert wines – and for making communion wines.

The best red – powerful, classic and full-bodied – comes from **Priorato**. Look for labels with angels on ladders or 'Scala Dei'. The **Ampurdán** makes good cherry-coloured ROSADOS and the light red VI NOVELL.

LA MANCHA AND VALDEPEÑAS
It takes hours and hours to drive across the great plains of **La Mancha**, a vast area containing half Spain's vineyards. The wine is rough – and deep yellow not white – and made from the Airén grape. However, a few (rather bland) bottles are blended for export.

Valdepeñas is a small wine area in the south almost enclosed by the larger La Mancha district. Here better quality wine is made and the huge *tinajas*, or Ali Baba wine jars, that stand by the roadside are actually used in the wine-making process. Traditionally, Valdepeñas is famous for ALOQUES: strong but light red wines, made from a blend of red and white grapes. Now

the better reds are made with fruity Cenibel, the best red Rioja grape (check on the label), and there are some oak-aged wines at Señoría de Los Llanos. Near **Toledo** the Marqués de Griñón makes fine Cabernet Sauvignon wines.

LEVANTE AND THE SOUTHEAST
The hot plains and hills of the southeast are Spain's largest producers of red wine: high–alcohol reds, with no acidity, which makes them taste very dull. **Alicante** reds are typical, though **Utiel-Requena** makes a lighter and more acid red and the area's best, most fragrant light ROSADA.

Jumilla produces dark, full-bodied and lethal reds, with an alcohol content of up to 18 per cent. SAVIN, Spain's biggest wine company, has a huge plant here, making a rather lighter and fresher *tinto*. Red **Yecla** is bigger-bodied, though a bit lower in alcohol. **Valencia** is Spain's chief wine port, and its local wine is white, the best being from Alto Turia.

However, if you want a refreshing, fruity local wine anywhere in southeast Spain, a good bet might be ROSADO, as many good rosés are made here.

Jerez wine cellar in Andalucía

THE SOUTHWEST

Many Spanish white wines taste remarkably like sherry. The hot sun produces sugar in the grape, which turns into dry alcohol. These wines may come as a surprise if you are not expecting them – but in Spain sherry is often the wine drunk with fish anyway. The white wines of **Extremadura** (try Cañamero and Chiclana, which is the white of Cádiz), fall into this category.

The best known of these wines comes from sherry's neighbouring district – **Montilla-Moriles** – and *amontillado* is derived from the town's name. There, high alcohol levels are achieved without fortifying

the wine, though fortified wines are also made. One of the best known *finos* in the south is Alvear's CB, and therefore is not in fact a sherry.

The **Condado de Huelva** is known for wines like sherry and GENEROSO, but increasingly it produces white table wines.

THE NORTHWEST AND CENTRAL NORTH

The cooler, wetter north of Spain is celebrated for fresh white wines, made in traditional ways from traditional Spanish grapes. In the Basque country they make TXACOLI on the sea coast: the white tastes of apples, is rather acid, and slightly *pétillant*.

In Galicia, there is also a small class of 'green' wines. Made in **Ribeiro** and the **Rías Baixas**, they differ from other wines in Spain in being more like German wines. Here the ALBARIÑO grape makes delicately fruity wines, which prickle slightly in the mouth. The red wine most drunk in Galicia is the fruity, light-coloured **El Bierzo**, from the south of the province. In Old Castile, **León** makes some good oak-aged reds, especially from the Palacio de Arganza, Look for the acronym VILE – they aren't, but avoid the black wines of Orense, which are. **Cigales**, long famous,

makes CLARETE by mixing black and white grapes. **Toro** is reputedly the oldest red wine in Spain – although the newest *Denonunación de Origen* district. Full-bodied with a hint of damson about it, the wine has a pleasantly lingering after-taste. Bodegas Fariña is the name to look for.

In the north of Old Castile, **Rueda** has had a boom in pleasant, fruity, young whites, which are not very alcoholic. It is a long-established white wine area, and they use the local and characterful Verdejo grape.

Both Marqués de Griñon and Marqués de Riscal (which make red wines elsewhere – Riscal in Rioja) make their white wines here, and they are some of the best in Spain.

Ribera del Duero, high up in the north of Old Castile, produces what is indisputably the most famous red wine in Spain, often 10 years in the barrel: Vega Sicilia. Younger, but still expensive, wines called Valbuena come from the same place. However, the local Ribera del Duero co-operative makes the affordable fruity Peñafiel wines. To the east, **Burgos** makes a light CLARETE.

Valdepañas red wines are fermented in amphora-like jars

Types of Wine

Spanish wine has immeasurably improved – and so has its reputation. There is now a vast amount of different types of wine produced in Spain. It is high alcohol stuff, often over 12 per cent and most of it is drunk young.

SHERRY

Sherry is one of the world's great white wines, and it is certainly the cheapest of them. It comes from Jerez, one of the few areas in Spain with a wine tradition to boast about. It is mainly made from the Palomino grape and blended on a SOLERA system of stacked barrels in huge buildings likened to 'sherry cathedrals'.

It is a fortified wine, and its high alcohol content has made it a before- or after-dinner wine, though in Spain *fino* is drunk as white wine. It is traditional in Spain to have a glass of *copa*, a glass of sherry, when eating *tapas*. Sherries are ranked for export by sweetness, though in Spain each category can vary quite widely. FINO and MANZANILLA are dry, AMONTILLADO is nutty and medium-dry, PALO CORTADO comes in sweetness between this and OLOROSO, which is a mature, and usually sweeter, sherry.

DESSERT WINES

Do not skip this part of the meal, even if you think you don't like sweet wine, for these are the true desserts of Spain.

Masia Bach's Extrésimo *blanco semi dulce* is rare in being both fresh-tasting yet honeyed, because most of Spain's other dessert wines are darker and much stronger.

Muscat is the main grape for dessert wines, often left to wrinkle and concentrate on the vine. In Alicante, the Roman Moscatel is one of the finest, while Moscatel de Valencia has a slight orange edge.

In the 18th century, **Málaga** *Dulce* was famous in Britain as 'Mountain Wine', and again in the 19th century in America.

Drinking it is like sipping sultanas. It certainly makes a much nicer end to a meal than a bad ice-cream. Smooth LÁGRIMA is the sweetest, Málaga Virgin the best known. Or try Scholtz Hermanos Solera 1885, which has a walnut scent.

VI RANCIOS are made in Alicante and **Tarragona** in a SOLERA system, for they are fortified dessert wines. Tarragona also makes *clásicos*, sweet wines, both red and white, and over a fifth alcohol!

CAVAS

CAVAS are light sparkling wines, made by the champagne method in **Penedès**, although the grapes may come from other DO *cava* areas. They mainly originate from San Sadurní de Nova where the big houses are based, including Codorníu, the largest champagne-style wine-maker in the world.

Freixenet Cordón Negro (in a black bottle) is also popular. The Spanish like their *cavas* on the sweet side. If you do not, look for *brut* or *brut natur*, which make a great aperitif. There are also lovely, but expensive, *champáns* made from Chardonay grapes. The best is from Codorníu, but a good alternative comes from Raimat.

YOUNG WINES

At home, Spaniards prefer to drink uncomplicated vino *corriente*. This is table wine, sold the first or second year after harvesting. These young reds are free of tannin, which would make ageing possible, so they taste fresh and fruity. As a result, they make remarkably pleasant – and pleasantly cheap – drinking. Even in Rioja, Spain's most famous wine area, only 40 per cent of the wine is aged in barrels.

The biggest BODEGA in Rioja is Campo Viejo, and their best seller in Spain is San Ascensio *2° año sin crianza* wine, which means 'sold in the second year after harvest, without wood ageing'. Another household brand of young red Rioja – Ernest Hemingway's favourite – is Banda Azul *3° año*, from Frederick Paternina, the country's largest exporter. The *3° año* from CUNE, another major firm, is also popular.

A–Z of Spanish Wine & Drink

A

Abocado
Semi-sweet table wine.

Agua helada
Iced water.

Agua mineral
Mineral water. It is sold everywhere, sparkling, *con gas*, or flat, *sin gas*. Some of it is bottled at famous spas like Lanjarón.

Agua potable
Drinking water.

Aguardiente
Any distilled liquor. The clear, *anís*-flavoured one is a favourite. *Aguardiente de orujo* is a rough grape brandy, like *marc*.

Aguja
Slightly sparkling.

Albariño ✪
The famous 'green' wine of Galicia, flowery but somewhat acid. Good with shellfish. It is made close to the Portuguese *vinho verde* region and from the same grape. It has a slight fizz as well, though the famous one from Palacio de Fefiñanes is still. However, you will still find them less sweet than *vino verde*.

Aloque
Red wine made from white grapes mixed with only ten per cent red ones. Light but surprsingly alcoholic wines.

Amontillado ✪✪✪
A famous style of sherry, amber-coloured, walnut flavoured and medium dry, though in Spain there are drier ones too. They are made from FINO, adding more wine spirit and maturing to become softer and darker. The best ones are old *finos* not suitable for drinking young.

Añejo
Old, mature or aged.

Anís ✪✪
One of Spain's favourite liqueurs, colourless, flavoured with aniseed and made all over the country. Much used for flavouring biscuits and desserts. There is a dry (*seco*) drunk with water as an aperitif, and sweet (*dulce*).

Año
Means 'year' and many popular wines are sold the second or third year after harvest.

B

Bebidas
A general word for drinks. But under this name come a series of sweet fruit *eaux de vie*, often in frosted bottles with names like *Bebidas de melecotón* (peach) and flavours like hazlenut. The Spanish also mix friut syrups with gin 'on the rocks'. Rives make flavours like passion fruit, pomegranate and the green kiwi.

Blanco, vino
White wines. In Spain these come in more varieties than they do in France. Many of them taste like sherry, particularly from the hot southwest and west. Then there are the aristocratic traditional white ones, that are aged in oak barrels. French-style white wines are made too, which are much crisper, fresh and fruity. There are a very few sweet white wines, but more sparkling wines, called CAVAS, and many golden dessert wines, from grapes like Muscat or Malvasía.

Blanco y negro ✪
Iced milk and coffee, scented with cinnamon.

Bodega
A wine store where wine and sherry are made, and so the company that makes the wine. Brands are very important in Spanish wine.

Brut, brut natur
Extra dry wine. This appears only on sparkling wine.

C

Café
Coffee. Brewed dark and strong in Spain. *Café solo* is black coffee in tiny cups, while *un corto* or *café cortado* is the identical amount of coffee served in a small tumbler with a little milk. *Café con leche* will be half milk to bring it to breakfast strength. *Descafeinado* is always instant decaffeinated. However, if you order iced coffee

Wine poured from a great height

(*café helado*) do not be surprised if a cup of coffee arrives with a glass of ice cubes. Pour the coffee on the cubes – it cools instantly.

Café en grano
Coffee beans (ready ground).

Carajillo, el ✪
A small black coffee with a shot of brandy or *anís* in it. A Catalan joke – the name means a 'willy'.

Castillo, castell
Château-bottled wines. There are comparitively few of these wines in Spain, which means all the grapes come from the estate. Good ones come from Marqués de Murrieta at Castel Ygay in Rioja, Torres Gran Viña Sol 'Green Label' at Castell de Fransola and Raimat in Penedès.

Cavas ✪✪
Spanish sparkling wines, made by the champagne method, when they acquire their sparkle in the bottle. Well worth trying if you avoid the sweet ones! Cordorníu is the world's largest producer.

Cepa
Grape.

Cerveza ✪
Spanish lager. As it is good with plenty of flavour, it is not worth paying for *cerveza extranerja* (imported beer). Try San Miguel *especial*, Águila, or Victoria brands. Majou is the best bitter and this is also less gassy.

Champán
Champagne-style. *Champaña* is French champagne.

Chocolate caliente ✪
Hot chocolate. Try it for breakfast, with crusty rolls to dip into it. The powder or tablets are sold with a thickener already added, and just need hot milk.

Clarete
As well as *vino tinto*, a second type of white wine is made, light enough to drink without food. Good ones are made in Valdepeñas, by mixing black and white grapes. Others are made in El Bierzo and Cigales in Old Castile, Valle de Montessey in the northwest, and Extremadura. They have no connection with French claret.

Coñac ✪✪
Brandy. An extremely popular after-dinner drink – and policemen on early-morning patrol have a shot with their breakfast coffee. Some brandies are smoother, in the

French fashion, while the roughish but grapey Fundador is liked by foreigners. However, Spaniards favour caramelised brandies, which are sweeeter and more perfumed. Veterano is one good brand and the smooth and aromatic Magno is popular.

Copitas
The tall, tulip-shaped glasses from which sherry is drunk. They narrow towards the top to hold the aroma.

Corriente, vino
A table wine sold the year of, or two years after, harvest. Most Spaniards drink this with their meals.

Cosecha
The year of harvest, given on the bottle. Most Spanish wine is drunk young, but the ageing of wine is regulated in three classes, with a minimum number of years for each class. A wine that is old for its class may be a good one, but red wine SIN CRIANZA, that is over three years, is a stale bottle.

Cremas
Sweet liquers. Ask ¿*Es en licor*? if in doubt. The best known orange liqueur (*crema de naranja*) is Curaçao in various colours including blue (*azul*). Triple Sec, which is less sticky, is worth trying. Others are crème de menthe (*crema de menta*) and coffee and chocolate liqueurs (*crema de café y crema de cacao*).

Cremat ✪✪
A potent Costa Brava coffee including brandy and rum, which are first flamed.

Crianza
'Aged in wood'. It is this that gives Spanish wines, and Rioja in particular, their distinctive Spanish taste. The barrels are made of oak, and new barrels make wine taste strongly of vanilla, so this is used, like spices in cooking, to flavour the wine.

The labelling laws specify how much time in the barrel each wine must have in each of the three cateogories: *crianza*, RESERVA and GRAN RESERVA. All whites and ROSADOS have a minimum of six months, reds one year, and red *Gran reservas* a minimum of two years.

Some companies decide to exceed the minimums, as part of the house style, which is why some old-fashioned Riojas have a strong whiff of vanilla. Others take the opposite path. The wine makers of Penedès decided to age most of their wines in bottles instead, which makes their wines taste more like French wines. The majority of Riojan whites are now not barrel-aged at all.

Crianza, sin
Most ordinary wines come into this class stored in vats, not barrels.

Cubalibre
Rum and coke or, in Spain, frequently gin and coke.

D

DO, Denominación de Origen
Similar to French *appellation contrôlée*, a designated quality control area.

Dulce
Sweet.

E

Embotellado por
Bottled for.

Espumoso
Any sparkling wine.

F

Fino
The best of the sherry styles, being dry, light and at around 17 per cent, the least alcoholic type. It is a blended wine, made in a SOLERA system. A small dose of alcoholic spirit is added to the young wine, which still allows a thick yeast, called *flor*, to develop on top. This protects the wine being oxidised by air above it. *Finos* are Spain's finest white wines and age well, but they also have qualities to make them perfect to drink young.

G

Gaseoso
Fizzy drink.

Generoso, un vino ✪
A fortified wine, drunk before or after a meal. Look for Condado Viejo de Huelva. They are also made in Rueda and the Ampurdán.

Ginebra
Gin, made by the huge firm of Larios. It is

often drunk short with ice and sweet mixers (see BEBIDAS) and with soda and lemon, *en pallofa*.

Gran reserva ✪✪✪
Much of Spain's best wine falls into this category and they are not expensive compared with matured French wines. In exceptional years, the wine-makers will earmark the vintage for preferential treatment. A *Gran reserva* may not be sold until the sixth year after harvest, and a red wine must spend a minimum of two years ageing in oak casks. White wines must spend at least six months in the casks. They are then moved to bottles to finish maturing.

Granvas
A sparkling wine made in tanks and so less good than a CAVA.

H

Hielo, con
With ice or 'on the rocks'.

Holandas
Not gin, but grape spirit, distilled in the

Decorative barrel used in the sherry producing area of Jerez

poorer parts of Spain and used to make sherry and brandy.

Horchata ✪
A creamy drink, sometimes iced, made from ground tiger nuts (see CHUFA in A–Z of Foods), sweetened with honey. It is sold freshly made in the south and Madrid.

I

Infusiones ✪
Herbal teas (also called *tisanas*) are very popular in Spain. Camomile is *manzanilla* (don't get it confused with the sherry), either bitter or sweet. Mint tea is *poleomenta*, *tila* is lime and *hierba luisa* is lemon verbena.

J

Jerez
Sherry, a mispronunciation of this place-name. It is a fortified wine drunk as an aperitif outside Spain. But Spainiards think of FINO as a dry white wine. It should be drunk from a half bottle, kept on ice.

Bringing in the grape harvest

Jugo de fruta
Fruit juice. *Pomelo, limón* and *naranja* are grapefruit, lemon and orange. *Manzana* and *piña* are apple and pineapple.

L

Lágrima, vino de ✪
Wine from 'tears', is juice from grapes that are so ripe that it drips without crushing. As a result the wines are old-gold, with a luscious sweet finish.

Leche
Milk. This is safe but homogenised, in UHT packs, so not particularly attractive to drink. One big firm, Puleva, also sells pasteurised milk in glass bottles, which makes a better cup of British tea. Flavoured milk is *un batido*.

Leche merengada ✪
A summer drink, and sometimes an ice, of milk with sweet meringue in it.

Licor ✪
Liqueur. They take the place of desserts to make a sweet finish to the meal. Two popular ones are the Catalan Calisay, a quinine-based, herbal liqueur with a sweetish aftertaste – good 'on the rocks'. Licor 43 (Cuarenta y tres) is clear orange in colour, vanilla flavoured and sweet, with a lingering finish.

Limonada
Sweet fizzy lemonade. Popular brands are Fanta, in one-person cans, and La Casera, a slightly lemony-tasting soda, used for diluting drinks.

M

Malvasía
A sweet dessert wine which takes its name from the grape that also makes Malmsey.

Manzanilla ✪✪✪
The driest and most delicate of pale-gold sherries. The taste comes from storing chosen light FINO sherries at Sanlúcar de Barrameda by the sea, where they pick up that faint salty tang. It has taken the name of camomile.

Manzanilla
Camomile. A popular herbal tea.

Mistela
Grape juice mixed with wine alcohol: an aperitif.

Moscatel ✪✪
The muscat grape gives its name to many sweet wines. In the south and Valencia, they are famous for their sultana taste, though the old ones often taste like toffee too. The best come from Málaga, though they are also made in Asturias and Penedès.

O

Oloroso ✪
A dark golden and the most full-bodied type of sherry. It is usually sweet and at least 18 per cent alcohol. All sherry starts off dry and develops in contact with the air – unlike wine. *Olorosos* are developed in a different SOLERA from FINOS. The new wine is fortified with more spirit at the beginning, and no yeast will grow on this. *Olorosos* mature by gradually oxidising. Good *olorosos* are reminiscent of port, though there are drier ones. 'Cream' sherry is made by adding juice from the Pedro Ximénez grape.

P

Pacharán ✪
The top generic liqueur in Spain. Made from sloes, red or brown, sweet and *anís*-flavoured, it is well worth trying 'on the rocks' before and after meals. Zoco is the best known brand.

Palo cortado ✪✪
A rarer type of sherry because it occurs by accident. It is darker than AMONTILLADO and in sweetness comes between it and OLOROSO.

Pedro Ximénez ✪
One of the sherry grapes, all of which start dry. But is also used for luscious dessert wines and its juice is added to OLOROSO, to make a 'cream' sherry.

Ponche ✪
In a silver bottle will be a herbalised old brandy: sweeter than ordinary brandy but less sticky than a liqueur. De Soto has a faint taste of orange. *Ponche* means 'punch' and includes drinks such as hot milk whisked with brandy and egg yolks.

Porrón
A wine bottle with a long spout for communal drinking without touching the mouthpiece.

Punys d'ous ✪
Menorca milk punch, which also contains rum, lemons, eggs and sugar.

Q

Queimada ✪✪✪
A powerful drink said to need three men – two to hold up the man who drinks it! Making it is a magic ritual in Galicia, where AGUARDIENTE DE ORUJO is poured in a bowl with sugar and apple slices or coffee beans and then flamed. Drinking starts when the flames die down.

R

Rancio, vi (vino) ✪
This mellowed dessert wine is fortified then aged in contact with the air, either in glass jars, left in the sun, or in a SOLERA of oak casks. The 20-year-old Fondillón is famous.

Refrescos
'Cool' drinks, implying soft ones.

Reserva ✪✪
These are the wines you are most likely to find back home – of reasonable quality, with some ageing. They are wines sold after harvest. Whites and ROSADOS have spent at least six months in oak casks, and reds at least a year, often much more. The result is a well balanced wine, with a satisfying after-taste. *Reservas* include both modest wines labelled only with the region, like a Navarra, and branded wines from companies in good areas like Rioja and Penedès.

Ron
Rum. Spain grows sugar cane and makes rum, dark rum and the famous colourless Bacardi (under licence), drunk simply with lemon juice and ice or as a CUBALIBRE, with coke.

Rosado ✪
Rosé wine. The ones from Navarra are well finished and *rosés* are also made in Aragón and Ribera del Duero. On the southeast coast, where the red wine is soupy and very

89

alcoholic, they are a good buy. Try the one made in Tarragona or the cherry-coloured *rosado* from Ampurdán. Utiel-Requena makes pale, refreshing ones.

S

Sangría ✪✪✪
The celebrated chilled wine punch dilutes the southern red wine, which is very high in alcohol, with citrus juice, ice and cold water – and adds a kick again with brandy. (See recipe page 116).

Seco
Dry.

Sidra ✪
Cider. Very popular in the Basque country, where *sidrerías* (cider shops) offer drink and food. Much drunk in Asturias.

Sifón
Soda water.

Sol y sombra ✪
'Sun and shade' is a hefty drink of sweet dark brandy, with a slug of *anís*.

Solera
The system in which sherries are blended. The name refers to a stack of barrels, often five rows high. New wine is first sorted by style – either a FINO or OLOROSO type. It is then put into the topmost barrel of a *solera* of the same group. As wine is taken from the older barrels, so they are each topped up from barrels of younger wine. *Fino* wine for sampling is drawn from the bottom row, by a little cup on a long stem, called a *venencia*, and then thrown in a great arc into a glass. The best and most expensive sherries come direct from the *solera*, without further blending.

T

Té con leche
Tea with milk. *Con limón* is with lemon. Iced tea is *té helado*.

Tinto, vino
Red wine. Usually a better bet in Spain.

Txacoli, chacoli ✪
The Basques are proud of this thin, rather acidic, white wine from vineyards by the sea. It has a faint taste of apples.

90

V

Verde, vino ✪
'Green wines'. These are the fresh whites of Galicia.

Vermú
Vermouth. A dry one with ice is *vermú blanco seco con hielo*, a popular lunchtime drink in Spain.

Vi novell
New wine. Modelled on *Beaujolais nouveau*, in Ampurdán.

Vino
Wine, pronounced with a soft B – 'bino'. A *viña* is a vineyard, while *vino de paso* is homemade raisin wine.

Vino de mesa, de pasto
Table wine.

Vino de Oporto
Port.

Vodka
Just as it looks. With tonic is *y tónica*.

W

Whisky americano
Bourbon.

Whisky sifón
Pronounced 'whicky', with soda.

Z

Zumo de fruta
Fruit juice Zumo de fruta.

Un jugo de naranja natural
Freshly-squeezed orange juice.

Zurracapote ✪
A hot red Rioja punch with cinnamon and brandy.

Zurro ✪
A white wine cooler from La Mancha.

Eating Out

Above: the cool interior of one of Levante's
restaurants
Right: try one of Spain's many fish restaurants

91

When & Where to Eat

Though Spaniards eat a light breakfast, you may want to stoke up with fruit and eggs, because lunch is normally eaten late. If you are going out to lunch, remember that Spaniards expect to eat between 14.00 and 16.00 hours – and this is the main meal of the Spanish day. Supper is then of the soup and eggs sort.

There is no shortage of cafés and bars in Spain. In simple *tascas* it is standing only but elsewhere you can sit. All have a choice of hot food.

Both smart *restaurantes* and the more modest *hosterías* (inns) may well offer local dishes (*platos típicos*) and there is surprisingly little difference between the types of dishes in the two places. The state-run tourist hotels, the *paradores*, have a policy of offering local food, often in historic buildings. At festivals and in mid-season these become busy, but normally they have room.

A *marisquería* specialises in shellfish, while a *merendero* is a casual outdoor eatery, often serving fish. Popular beaches also have *tascas* serving drinks and some food. The modest roadside *venta* (which means 'sale') usually sells hot food as well as drinks and ices.

For afternoon tea, many *pastelerías* (pastry shops) also have a few tables; while you might find a *salón de té*. *Cafés* specialise in coffee, beer and ice-creams rather than food.

EATING THROUGH THE DAY
A bar is the place to buy breakfast in Spain, usually a quick affair of coffee and bread, though some specialise in chocolate and CHURROS. Early risers may then have a snack mid-morning, for lunch is late, rarely before 14.00 hours and often as late as 16.00 hours. Children have a *merienda*, (snack) when they come home from school, and adults may have a beer or pastry. *Tapas* (bar snacks) start about 19.00 hours, to fill in time before dinner or supper, This will be a lighter meal, eaten around 21.00 hours at home or in the country in the north. The south keeps later hours, 22.00 or 23.00 hours in town, and later still in Madrid.

EATING TAPAS
Tapas (bar snacks) are served with all drinks. They used to be free, and marinated olives and salted nuts may still be 'on the house', but you will have to pay for other snacks.

Cheese, raw ham and CHORIZO on bread are basic, as is cold potato ENSALADILLA and fried squid (CALAMARES) in the south. Prawns are universal (and expensive) and on the north coast there will be potted crab and clams and mussels in wine. Fried fish is popular in the south – try shark in batter (CAZÓN). All sorts of good things are deep fried – croquettes and cheesy puffs with vegetables or ham. Then there are varieties of things in sauce, like meatballs and tripe (CALLOS). Finally there is chicken in garlic and miniature pork kebabs (PINCHOS) whose name is used to mean a *tapa*.

In popular bars a selection is laid out under glass. *Vamos de pinchos* means 'We're going out looking for *tapas*'– a *tapas* crawl! For just a tiny sample, ask for *una tapa*. *Una ración* is a more substantial portion, enough for two or three to share – and a cheap way of eating out quickly.

Eating alfresco in Seville

At the Restaurant

Restaurant meals are usually leisurely. If you are in any sort of hurry, the set menu will come faster. Cooking methods in Spain tend to be straight-forward, portions are enormous and almost everything is served with bread to mop up the juices – though your plate may end up covered with bones from either meat or fish. There is very little highly spiced food.

Soup or salads, then egg dishes or vegetables, are served as separate courses before the main course.

A popular soup is made of shellfish (*sopa de mariscos*). Soup may be based on clear broth from the stockpot (*caldo*) or may be a *potaje*, thick with vegetables. *Sopa de cebollas, espárragos or champiñones* (onion, asparagus or mushroom soup) is just as likely to be canned as it is at home.

Entremés de carne is a selection of cold meats, but *ensalada mixta*, salad with tomato and tuna, is one of the most popular starters. Salads are put on the table before the main course, rather than after it, or as side dishes.

Egg dishes such as TORTILLA, which is not an omelette but more like a cake of egg, and HUEVOS A LA FLAMENCA, eggs in a wonderful mixed vegetable sauce (see recipes pages 102), make a main dish if you are not hungry. PAELLA and pasta dishes are also considered starters. Vegetable dishes tend to be massive, while the bean dishes are soupy stews, with plenty of liquid and a meal in themselves.

Fish cooked *a la plancha* is from the griddle, *a la parrilla* it is grilled (often on charcoal), while *la barbacoa* means an outside grill. If you prefer fish with sauce, try MERLUZA EN SALSA VERDE, or A LA VASCA (see recipe page 109). Meat, poultry and fish used to be served by themselves, with

An inviting entry to a smart Spanish restaurant where local dishes are usually on the menu

bread, though now many dishes come with potato chips. Fried and roast chicken (*pollo frito* or *asado*) and pork chops (*chuletas de cerdo*) are universal. But lamb chops (*chuletas de cordero*) are more of a luxury, If the restaurant advertises its oven outside, *un horno* (an old-fashioned bread oven), the roast lamb will be a real treat. *Una caldereta* is a stew.

Spaniards mainly close a meal with fruit; in general the desserts, pastries and ice-creams are not good. However, the classics like CREMA CATALANA and TOCINO DE CIELO can be delicious and are worth trying once. The cheese selections are not large, while soft cheeses may be served with honey or sugar as a dessert. A finishing sweet touch to a meal is more likely to come from a COÑAC (brandy) which is usually sweet and often perfumed.

HAVING A DRINK

Spaniards make an occasion of pre-dinner drinking. but if you order white wine before dinner, you will probably be brought sherry. Apart from beer and sherry, sweet drinks such as vermouth on ice or the *anís*-flavoured, brandy-like PACHARÁN are popular aperitifs. Gin is also served with sweet mixer-syrups. Mineral water or even GASEOSO, a fizzy lemonade, are used to dilute the wine.

At the end of the meal, both men and women enjoy sweet liqueurs. When ordering brandy (COÑAC), you will always be asked which you prefer: some are sweet and perfumed and others resemble French *cognacs*.

PAYING THE BILL

You are unlikely to be hurried through your meal, and the bill will come only when you ask. Some places include service on the bill. There is no fixed rate for tipping in restaurants, although generally 5–10 per cent of the bill is appreciated. Some people leave a pile of whatever small coins they have in their pockets.

Special Requirements

When arriving at a restaurant, if you have any special diet requirements be sure to indicate this to the waiters and they will do their best to help.

VEGETARIANS

Spanish food is largely peasant cooking, based on good vegetables. Many restaurants have pictures of dishes outside. However, vegetarians should beware! Many soups, vegetable dishes and PAELLAS contain small amounts of bacon or sausage. There is also a tradition of cooking in pork fat. The only way to find out is to ask.

Another thing to beware of is CUAJADA, which looks like yoghurt; it is junket, and so set with animal rennet (*cuaja*).

Many pastries are, or used to be, made with lard.

GLUTEN-FREE DIET

Bread is the accompaniment to every Spanish meal, as meat, fish and poultry are normally served without vegetables. Ask for a side order of boiled potatoes (*un ración de patatas hervidas*) though it will be easier to get chips (*patatas fritas*). The good news is that there are many dishes that are not flour-based, particularly grills and rice.

Flour is used in wine-based sauces. Bread is commonly used in soups as a thickener, and is puréed for sauces, particularly those that contain nuts.

Among *tapas*, avoid the Basque *bola*, which is a béchamel-based croquette and all BUÑUELOS: many are based on choux pastry. Cocoa is sold mixed with a flour thickener.

MILK-FREE DIET

Milk has a low standing in the Spanish kitchen, being kept for young children. Cream is not much used either, except in the north. Avoid wine-cream sauces, but the majority of creamy puddings are based on eggs or ground almonds.

CHILDREN

Spanish children eat out in restaurants with their parents from their early years, and so they learn how to behave considerately. Children are welcomed everywhere except, perhaps, in the smartest of restaurants. The portions in Spain are enormous, so most small children eat off their mother's plate.

Finding food for children is not difficult, because the *tapas* dishes sold in bars are ideal for the young. Most children like CALAMARES (squid rings) which look vaguely like pasta, while dishes like meatballs in tomato sauce are universal. Don't be put off by sherry sauces – the cooking process destroys the alcohol. Fried fish is of better quality than elsewhere – with the ever-popular chips.

Hamburguesas (hamburgers) are not recommended.

For breakfast try hot chocolate, for Spanish milk is homogenised and not particularly pleasant to drink. Nesquik is good for cold chocolate drinks.

Cafés and bars are open at lunch and before the late supper hours of Spain. However, it is preferable to feed children around 18.30 hours – not when bars are full of men having a drink after work.

Vegetarians will find many appetizing dishes on offer

Eating
In

Above: *feast your eyes on a Spanish street market*
Right: *Buen apetito en España!*

Shopping

Supermarkets have come to Spain in a big way, but you will also find many corner stores, specialist food shops and lots of lively street markets.

If you can find a market, or if you go to a *Hiper* or a *Pryca* (vast supermarkets) early in your visit, bulk shopping will save you a lot of money. Equally, don't be embarrassed about buying in very small quantities. Spanish people point and often buy l00g (¼1b) at a time.

Un almacén is a big store, *una tienda de comestibles* a food shop and *una mantequería* is a general grocery. *La panadería* sells only bread, but in *una pastelería* you can get sweet breakfast rolls as well as cakes and biscuits. Your children may pester you to stop at *una bombonería*, sweet stall.

You will find most of the items you buy at home in Spanish supermarkets – with small differences. For instance, canned tomato comes in three convenient ways. *Tomato pelado* are whole tomatoes, while *tomate triturado* is minced and *tomato frito* is a thick tomato sauce, which drowns everything if you use too much. And don't buy TOCINO if you want breakfast bacon. This is solid fat from the pork belly, with no lean, and it is for chopping and frying with vegetables. Ask for *beicón*. Butter quickly loses its pleasant taste; margarine, sold in tubs, makes a better spread.

MEAT AND POULTRY

As well as the useful 'spit-roast chicken' stalls found in large villages at the weekend, Spain has special shops, called *pollerías* for selling chickens and eggs. Most supermarkets and butchers also sell fresh and frozen chicken.

A meat shop, *una carnicería*, looked rather medieval until recently, with lumps of meat on hooks. Supermarkets still cut meat to order. Spaniards eat quite a lot of mince, in meat-balls and stuffed vegetables. Try the less-familiar veal mince, or a mixture with pork or ham.

By the way, meat from the bullfight is not sold in ordinary butchers (see CARNE DE LIDIA).

Ternera is a cross between beef and veal, and makes good chops and steaks. However, most families eat pork as their main meal. Small village shops often have a chilled cabinet with chops and a boned loin or pork for slicing. Lamb is a luxury, and chops most of all. Stewing lamb is sold with all the bones in, but is good. In the south, kebab meat is sold ready-cubed and marinated.

Raw ham is used a lot in Spanish recipes. The cheapest type of SERRANO (off the bone) is in the cabinet with the cold meat and a bit will be cut to order for you.

Think of red CHORIZO as a sausage with ketchup already in it. It is much more meaty than British sausages. The ones with red string are often very hot (*picante*) while white string means they are mild. The whitish BUTIFARRA is made from veal and pork, for grilling, while LONGANIZA and black puddings like MORCILLA are for cutting up and flavouring bean dishes.

You will also find a 'deli' section in most large butchers, selling cooked and ready-to-eat cured meat.

FISH

The Spanish love fish and eat it about three times a week. Spain has some of the best fish in Europe; it is sold fresh everywhere and there is a considerable choice. In the Cádiz area there are also *freidurías* take-away fried fish shops.

Spain is very regional: fish are called different names in different places, while one name can be used for several different fish. Fish are sorted by size – confusing, until you realise the same fish appears in different piles. Tiny sardines under 2cm (¾in) long are for deep frying, and the normal-size ones for grilling. Larger hake (*merluza*) are for cooking, but little ones (*pescadillas*) are for

A well-stocked market stall to tempt the shopper

The Spanish enjoy a wide range of good fresh fish and seafood

chopping up to make fish soup, Unsorted (mixed) prawns can be cheaper than sorted ones.

Basically, oily fish like mackerel are best grilled. If they look like meat steaks, such as swordfish or tuna, they need lots of oil while grilling. Pinkish fleshed fish, sold skinned, need an acid marinade, or lemon juice and capers to serve. White fish can be cooked every way.

Grilling is easiest, while barbecuing is more fun if you have outside space for a fire. Frying is easy for two, but hard work for more people, because there are rarely enough pans, or space, in a Spanish kitchen.

Many Spanish recipes start fish in the pan and finish in the oven with a sauce. A thick fish soup is also a good bet. Shellfish are sold raw and prawns need boiling – 3 minutes for *gambas* and 5 or 6 for *langostinos* and *cigalas*, depending on size. They are good eaten with coarse salt. Big ones can be

barbecued. Bigger clams are usually eaten raw, little ones included in soups and sauces.

Small freezer shops are common in villages and these stock open boxes of fish and also different vegetables. Here you can buy quantities as small as l00g (¼1b) to go in something like a *paella*. They also offer items like battered crab claws, fish in crumbs and little salted cod pies (*tortas de bacalao*). Don't buy BACALAO (salted cod) unless you can wait a day for it to soak. After that, it can be used like fresh fish. Salted sardines are sold packed in a fan shape in wooden boxes: rinse and use them. Many classic dishes, such as *bacalao a la purrusalda* (leek and salted cod soup) are also canned.

CHEESE

The national cheeses are mainly hard and cheddar-like – and something of an acquired taste. MANCHEGO is the famous name and there are many other cheeses like it. An old, ripened cheese (*añejo*) will be very strong, crumbly and hard, a bit like Parmesan. The same cheese is softer and blander when young (*queso tierno*). You may be asked *¿Queso de vaca o queso de cabra?*, Cows' milk cheese or goats'? as the country is famous for its sheep and goat cheeses. These are mainly hard or semi-hard cheeses too, all cut in slices from a drum-shape, and the main difference is that cows' milk cheese is a bit cheaper. Bland international cheeses like Edam are also widely sold. Firm Spanish cheeses grate well and the most successful cooked dish is *queso frito* – slices egged and crumbed, then fried. They are popular to start or end the meal.

Many areas do make soft fresh cheeses, but they are not so easy to find; nor is cottage cheese, REQUESÓN. Soft CUAJADA (junket) is more widely distributed. Several cheeses are described in the A–Z of Spanish Food.

VEGETABLES AND FRUIT
You will find a good choice of vegetables in markets and in *una verdulería*, a green-grocer. The quality is exceptionally good, sizes are huge, colours bright and prices low.

Learn to use the vegetables available. Chard, with leaves like spinach, is worth a try, and whole artichokes, too. Look up how to eat them in the A–Z of Spanish Food if they are not familiar and then try them out. In summer, Spaniards love salads.

PICNICS
The salads in Spain are so delicious and varied that shopping for picnics is a positive pleasure.

The *bocadillo* is one of the nicest sandwiches in the world. Made from a crusty roll, it is split and dribbled with olive oil, instead of butter, which goes off quickly in hot weather. Inside, ham (SERRANO) and cheese are a wonderful combination. PA AMB TOMÀQUET, Catalan bread with tomato juice pressed in, is also very good.

There are many other picnic ingredients to choose from. Little cans full of seafood, sold for starters, are particularly good with salad, for example. Vegetables in marinade, eaten with a spoon from the can, are excellent. Two of you can easily finish a can.

Many cans have ring-pull openers, but the big litre beer bottles will require a bottle opener!

COOKED MEAT
You will find cold meat in supermarkets or in a specialist *charcutería*. They sell the familiar salamis and mortadellas and Spanish cold meats. The largest CHORIZOS, about 5cm (2in) across, are for slicing and eating raw. Many pressed meats are made, half minced, half in small pieces. *Pudín de cerdo* is rather like corned beef made of pork.

Spaniards eat a lot of ham. The most expensive is raw SERRANO. But cooked ham is sold everywhere, while cured 'ham' pieces of shoulder are good and much cheaper.

Colourful fresh produce in its infinite variety

Recipes

The recipes below vary in difficulty. Those with one star (✪) are simple to prepare, while those with two stars (✪✪) are more complex and time consuming.

HUEVOS A LA FLAMENCA

BAKED EGGS WITH GYPSY TRIMMINGS
✪✪

SERVES FOUR

Slices of sausage, bits of ham and prawns can all go into this dish – all together, if you like – for it is a colourful mixture of whatever comes to hand, baked in tomato sauce.

4 tablespoons olive oil
1 large onion, peeled and chopped
2 garlic cloves, skinned and finely chopped
2 *chorizo* sausages, sliced
100g/4oz slice raw *serrano* ham, diced
1 large green pepper, destalked, seeded and diced
400g/14oz can tomatoes and juice
salt, pepper and paprika
100g/4oz cooked green beans, cut into short lengths
4 or 8 eggs

Heat the oven to high for butane gas (180°C, 350°F, gas mark 4 at home) and put in a *cazuela* or four ovenproof baking dishes. Heat the oil in a frying pan and fry the onions slowly until soft, then add the garlic. Fry the sausage and ham in the pan until cooked. Distribute them between the dish(es) in the oven.

Add the diced pepper to the pan and fry for 3 to 4 minutes. Empty the tomatoes into the pan, breaking them up with a spoon. Season with salt, pepper and a little paprika and cook until the tomato reduces to a sauce. Add the beans and heat through.

Spoon the vegetable sauce over the sausage and ham. Break in one or two eggs per person, then just swirl them lightly into the sauce with a fork. Bake in the oven for about 15 minutes until the eggs are just set. Eat with bread and a green salad.

Note. At home you can use smoked gammon cut from a knuckle, which is cheap, instead of *serrano*. Chicken livers go well in it too.

TORTILLA DE CAMARONES

SPANISH SHRIMP OMELETTE
✪✪

SERVES FOUR

Spanish omelettes are not like French ones, but more like cakes - the shape of a sponge layer. They are often cut like cakes, too, into wedges that go into sandwiches, or are spiked with cocktail sticks, as tapas. A variety of things can go in them, cooked potato and fried onion being popular. But shrimps and srnall prawns almost always end up in fritters or tortillas, as they are too small to peel for a fish dish. Remember, in Spain they are raw, so need brief cooking.

300–350g/10–12oz raw shrimps or prawns
4 tablespoons olive oil
2 tablespoons chopped onion
1 small garlic clove, skinned and finely chopped
salt, pepper and paprika
8 large eggs

Start by peeling the shrimps – or delegate the job! Meanwhile heat 2 tablespoons of the oil in a frying pan, about 23cm/9 inches across, and fry the onion slowly until soft, adding the garlic at the end. Turn up the heat

and add the shrimps. Cook for 2 minutes, stirring occasionally, then sprinkle with salt, pepper and paprika. Turn them into a large bowl.

Wipe the pan with kitchen paper and heat the remaining oil. Break the eggs on to the shrimps and stir together. Pour the egg mixture into the pan, distributing the shrimps well. Cook for I minute over high heat to set the bottom, then turn down to low. Use a spatula to pull the egg away from the side of

Ingredients for shrimp tortilla

the pan and make a straight side. To make sure the bottom is not sticking, shake the pan by pushing it away then pulling it back vigorously. When the top starts to set, cover it with a plate and flip the pan over, to turn out the *tortifla.* Slide it back the other way up, and give it 2 to 3 more minutes to set. *Tortilla* should be quite chunky and solid. You can eat it with tomato sauce if you like.

ENTREMESES ESPECIALIDADES

THREE SPECIAL STARTER SALADS
⭐

Salads are the backbone of summer lunches. Nice though tomato salad and lettuce are, it is a treat to have something special.

PIMIENTOS CON ANCHOAS

PIMENTOS WITH ANCHOVY

Buy a couple of cans each of red pimentos and anchovies. Drain them both. Cut the pimentos into strips. Arrange on a plate and crisscross with anchovies. Good with cold cooked beans in tomato sauce – which can also be bought canned.

Potato and tuna salad

ALCACHOFAS Y ATÚN

ARTICHOKE HEARTS WITH TUNA

Tiny fluffy artichoke hearts (not the bases) are sold canned and frozen (the latter need brief cooking). Split them lengthways into three, and serve with canned tuna, mayonnaise and cold potatoes.

PAN Y TOMATE CON CHORIZO

TOMATO–BREAD WITH CHORIZO

The Catalans are so fond of this that I have included it, even though it seems too simple. Buy good crusty bread and cut into rounds. Cut ripe tomatoes in half, then crush on to the bread, so it becomes soaked with the juice. Dribble with a little olive oil: some people rub with a garlic clove, too. Top these with thin slices of CHORIZO which is sold for eating raw or SALCHICHÓN which has peppercorns in it.

GARBANZOS EN SALSA DE TOMATE

CHICK-PEAS IN TOMATO SAUCE
✪✪

SERVES FOUR

Chick-peas look a little like hazelnuts when they have been soaked, and have a bit of a nutty taste too. This basic recipe goes well with fried or grilled sausages, while you try out the local chorizos and butifarras, to discover which ones you prefer. A little chopped serrano, or pancetta, which is like streaky bacon, is good fried in it with the onion. You can eat this stew cold with salad, or put it into a tortilla (see recipe on page 102). Or eat chick-peas a favourite Spanish way, with hot cooked spinach stirred in.

500g/1lb dried chick-peas (or lkg/2lb ready-soaked)
2 tablespoons olive oil
1 mild Spanish onion, peeled and chopped
1 green pepper, destalked, seeded and chopped
2 garlic cloves, skinned and finely chopped
800g/1lb 12oz can whole or chopped tomatoes
l tablespoon paprika
2 tablespoons wine vinegar
pepper and salt

Soak the chick-peas overnight, if necessary (see note). Heat the oil in a flameproof casserole and gently fry the onion until soft, adding the green pepper and garlic towards the end. Add the tomatoes and their juice, chopping them a little with a spoon, if they are whole. Add the soaked chick-peas. Stir in the paprika and vinegar, and add pepper to taste. Bring to the boil, cover and simmer, stirring occasionally. Spanish chick-peas cook in about an hour (at home Greek chick-peas need 2 hours), but longer won't hurt them, and they reheat well. Check occasionally to see that they are still covered with liquid and stir. Add salt to taste before serving.

Note. In Spain, chick-peas are sold ready-soaked on delicatessen counters. But there are two ways to soak them yourself. Either cover the chick-peas well with three times the volume of cold water and leave overnight. Or pour boiling water over them and leave for one hour.

ENSALADILLA DE PATATAS Y ATÚN

POTATO SALAD WITH TUNA AND CAPERS
✪

SERVES FOUR

The secret of really good potato salad is to make it then eat it straight away, when the potatoes are still slightly warm. Any potato left over makes an extra item in a mixed salad. The Spanish invented anchovy-stuffed hard-boiled eggs, and these go well with it.

1kg/2lb new potatoes
¼ mild Spanish onion
2 (100g/4oz) cans tuna in oil
salt and pepper
300ml/½ pint mayonnaise
2 tablespoons drained capers

If the potatoes are small, boil them in their skins until cooked. If they are large, peel and cut into equal size chunks and cook, then drain well in a colander. Peel as soon as they are cool enough to handle and chop into a shallow salad bowl. Chop the onion and scatter over the potatoes. Empty the tuna and its oil into the potatoes and break up the fish with a fork. Sprinkle with salt and pepper and turn gently. Add enough mayonnaise to coat the potatoes to your taste, then sprinkle with capers and serve.

ALCACHOFAS SALTEADAS CON JAMÓN

SAUTÉED ARTICHOKE BASES WITH HAM
✪✪

SERVES FOUR

Artichokes are always in the market, but many people don't know what to do with them, or find them fiddly to eat whole. This is an easy way to eat them fresh. You can also make this popular dish with canned (and in Spain frozen) bases, or cooked broad beans or fresh peas. At home a 500g/1lb bag of frozen broad beans is perfect. Buy the cheaper serrano ham for cooking, not the best slices, which are carved from the bone for tapas.

8 globe artichokes
2 tablespoons olive oil
1 onion, peeled and finely chopped
2 garlic cloves, skinned and finely chopped
250g/8oz raw *serrano* ham *para cocinar*, cubed
salt and pepper
chopped fresh parsley (optional)

To prepare the artichokes, chop off the stalks (if they are stringy, that means the artichokes are tough and will need an extra 5 minutes' cooking). Trim the bottom so it is flat, removing small leaves. Turn on its side and cut through the top leaves, leaving a base about 4cm/1½ inches deep. Trim away the side leaves with a small knife until the white base shows through. Cook the bases in boiling salted water for 10 minutes. Drain upside down and cool briefly.

Flip off any soft leaf stumps with your thumb, revealing the choke. Use a spoon and your thumb to remove and discard the bristly choke, leaving a smooth saucer-shaped base. The bases need about 5 minutes' more cooking, either in a frying pan (as in this dish), or in boiling water if you want to use them for salad.

Heat the oil in a frying pan and cook the onion until softened, adding the garlic near

Artichokes with ham

the end. Add the ham, tossing over high heat for 1 to 2 minutes. Quarter the artichoke bases, add them to the pan and fry for about 5 minutes, stirring occasionally, Season and serve garnished with parsley, if you can buy it.

SOPA DE PESCADO Y MARISCOS CON NARANJAS

FISH SOUP WITH ORANGE
✪✪

SERVES FOUR

Many people don't like bones on their plates, so this is a good way to serve only the fillets, yet use the heads, bones and skins that you have paid for. It is also fun to eat and to shop for. Look at the fish as you are buying them and imagine that about one third (from the middle of the back) will be bone-free white flesh, and the rest can go to make the soup part. Get the fishmonger to do the chopping for you: 'limpieles, por favor'.'

Shellfish that look interesting but fiddly to open, can go in and will be no problem. The stalks (not heads) of parsley can go in too,

Fish soup with orange

and also any of those recognisable herbs that get picked on holiday walks because they smell nice.

2kg/4½lb mixed fish with heads
2 large Spanish onions, peeled and chopped
2 bay leaves
small bunch parsley
handful of herbs, even wild lavender
2 tablespoons olive oil
I green pepper, destalked, seeded and chopped
2 large garlic cloves, skinned and finely chopped
2 tablespoons flour
200ml/7fl oz dry white wine
salt, pepper and paprika
your choice of: 200g/7oz prawns and/or little clams, small crabs, etc
1 large tomato, skinned and seeded, flesh chopped
½ dried chilli (*guindilla*) or a little cayenne
8 small new potatoes (optional)
1 orange

Identify the best bits of the fish and chop these out quickly, if this hasn't been done. No need to be fussy about this, as all the rest is used. Keep the flesh aside on a plate.

Put the heads, bones, skin, etc in a large saucepan or flameproof casserole with 1 chopped onion and the bay leaves. Cut off and scrunch up the parsley stalks and add them and any herbs. Cover with 1.2 litres/2 pints water and bring to the boil. Simmer for 40 minutes, then strain off the stock.

Heat the oil in a pan, large enough to take everything and fry the remaining onion slowly until soft. Add the chopped pepper, then the garlic.

Sprinkle with flour and cook for 1 minute, stirring, then add the wine. Season the reserved fish pieces with salt, pepper and paprika and tuck these into the pan, with any little crabs, prawns, clams, etc. Add the chopped tomato flesh and chilli and potatoes (if using). These should be small or cubed to the size of big marbles. Cut the zest from the orange in a spiral with a potato peeler and add.

Squeeze the orange juice. Pour in 1 litre/1¾ pints fish stock and bring to simmering point. Cover and cook over low heat for 20 minutes, then add the orange juice. Check the seasoning and add parsley.

Note. For a party at home, the stock can be strained off and 2 tablespoons rice cooked in it. Serve this first, garnished with chopped prawns and parsley. Serve the fish with boiled new potatoes as a main course.

CIGALAS A LA PARRILLA CON ALIOLI

GRILLED SCAMPI WITH GARLIC MAYONNAISE
✪✪

Serves four

This is messy to eat, so a good dish to serve when everyone is in bathing suits. The sauce is very strong – not for anyone who does not like garlic. It is the best accompaniment for grills, and Spaniards serve it with grilled lamb chops and roast lamb.

1kg/2lb raw scampi without heads
a little olive oil
coarse salt
For the *alioli*:
6 garlic cloves, skinned
½ teaspoon salt
2 egg yolks
200ml/7fl oz good olive oil

Make the *alioli* first. Chop the garlic really finely, then sprinkle with the salt. Use the flat side of a table knife to mash it to a paste – or use a pestle and mortar. Put the egg yolks in a bowl and stir in the garlic.

In a Spanish kitchen there is no danger of cold oil, but if you are at home, stand the jug of measured oil in a pan of warm water for a few minutes. Whisk the egg yolks, preferably with an electric whisk, and add a few drops of oil. When these have been incorporated, add a few more – the mayonnaise should thicken quickly. As soon as it thickens, you can start adding the oil faster, beating all the time, until it is incorporated. If you keep the sauce in the refrigerator, place in a screw-top jar or keep well covered.

Light the barbecue and let the fire die down, or heat the grill to high. Brush the scampi with oil and grill for about 8–10 minutes, depending on their size. Transfer them to a dish and scatter with coarse salt.

The neat way to get scampi out of their shells is to pick one up from the back and press the sides together. This cracks the shell all down the stomach. You can get a thumb under the legs on one side and peel them upwards, to take off a bit of the back shell – like taking off a saddle. After that, pinch the tail fin hard and pull the body. It should pop out when the vacuum is released. To eat, dunk the scampi in the sauce. Plenty of serviettes will be needed.

MERLUZA A LA VASCA

HAKE IN WINE AND SEAFOOD SAUCE
✪✪

SERVES FOUR

Any white fish can be used for this dish, which is liked by children, because the fish doesn't have too many bones, It is finished in the oven, and you can use a big cazuela or one ovenproof dish per person, which is easier. It is good, too, with frozen peas substituted for the shellfish, but be sure then to include the parsley.

4 tablespoons olive oil
250g/8oz onions, peeled and chopped
2 big garlic cloves, skinned and finely chopped
4 tablespoons flour
salt and pepper
I teaspoon paprika
4 hake steaks or fish fillets, 700g/1½lb
I medium tomato
300ml/½pint dry white wine
200ml/7fl oz water with a fish cube, or fish stock
1 bay leaf
250g/8oz baby clams or prawns, peeled
chopped fresh parsley to garnish (optional)

Heat the oven to high for butane gas (18°C, 350°F, gas mark 4 at home). Heat the oil in a frying pan and fry the onions slowly until soft, then add the garlic. Put the flour on a plate and sprinkle with salt, pepper and paprika. Take any loose bones out of the fish, then coat the pieces in the seasoned flour. Push the onion to the sides of the pan and put in the fish, frying it until golden – about 4 minutes each side. Transfer the fish pieces to an oven proof dish or dishes and put them in the oven.

Peel the tomato while the fish is frying: ripe skin should strip of easily. Quarter it, then scoop out and discard the seeds. Chop the flesh and add to the pan with a little of the wine. Reduce this, stirring occasionally. Add the remaining wine and water (or stock) and crumbled stock cube if using, plus the bay leaf, and bring back to the boil. Pour over the fish. If individual dishes are being used, you may need a little more liquid. Tuck the clams or prawns round the fish pieces and return to the oven. Reduce the oven temperature (to 160°C, 325°F, gas mark 3 at home) and leave the dish for 10 minutes or so. Serve sprinkled with parsley and eat with crusty bread.

PAELLA VALENCIANA

MIXED RICE WITH CHICKEN AND SEAFOOD
✪✪

SERVES FOUR

Eat paella in a restaurant when you are in Spain: they have the pans and space. It is quite hard work to prepare yourself. However, you must have a recipe to take home, to remind you of your holiday. Best to take the rice home too. This is the easy version, but even so it takes over an hour.

4–5 tablespoons olive oil
I onion, peeled and chopped

2 garlic cloves, skinned and finely chopped
700ml/1 pint 4fl oz good stock
200ml/7fl oz dry white wine
30 saffron strands or 2g sachet saffron powder
250g/8oz little squid (or mussels, cleaned)
250g/8oz raw prawns, peeled
salt, pepper and cayenne
4 chicken thighs, or 2 legs, split in half
400g/14oz Spanish medium-grain rice (or Italian risotto rice)
1 teaspoon paprika
I00g/4oz cooked green beans or peas
200g/7oz canned red pimento, drained
chopped fresh parsley

Use two pans to speed frying – a *paella* or wide shallow flameproof casserole big enough to take the complete dish, plus a frying pan. Heat 2 tablespoons of oil in the *paella* pan and fry the onion gently until soft, adding the garlic at the end.

Next, warm the stock and wine, then pour a little of this liquid over the saffron in a cup.

Prepare the shellfish. To clean squid, first use the tentacles to pull out everything inside, then cut off the heads above the eyes. Discard everything except the tentacles and body. Flex the body to pop out the transparent 'spine'. Wash well, rubbing off the skin, and cut the body into rings.

Heat 2 more tablespoons oil in the second pan and put in the squid tentacles and rings. Fry for a couple of minutes, then remove to a plate. Put in the peeled prawns and fry for 2 minutes, then transfer to the plate with the squid. Rub salt, pepper and cayenne into the chicken pieces. Add more oil to the pan if necessary, then add the chicken pieces and fry for about 10 minutes on each side. Meanwhile, wash the rice in a sieve and drain. When the onion is ready, add the rice to the *paella* pan and stir into the

The classic dish of Spain: Paella

onion. Fry for a couple of minutes, stirring, then sprinkle with the paprika. Add the saffron liquid and one-third of the stock and bring to the boil. Start timing now – for 20 minutes. When the liquid has been absorbed, add another third of the stock and evenly distribute the chicken, squid, prawns and beans or peas round the *paella* pan.

When the liquid has nearly gone, add the remaining liquid and give the mixture a stir. Move the chicken pieces, bedding them into the liquid round the pan. The liquid should all disappear, and cooking time should be up about 6 to 7 minutes later. Test that the rice is cooked. Cut the pimento into strips and lay these across the rice. Turn off the heat and wrap the *paella* pan in foil then newspaper, to keep in the steam. Let it stand for 10 minutes. The flavours will blend and the last drop of liquid should disappear. Sprinkle with parsley and serve. Spaniards prefer red wine with *paella*.

Note. Packs of small, frozen squid are often sold in larger supermarkets in the UK.

POLLO AL CHILINDRÓN

FRIED CHICKEN AND HAM AND RED PEPPERS
✪✪

SERVES FOUR

This is Spain's most popular fried chicken dish, named after a card game. It might seem extra trouble grilling the peppers, but it fits in nicely with the frying time. Cooked like this they are a basic Spanish ingredient, sweet and juicy, and make a lovely puréed sauce.

2 red peppers
2 tablespoons olive oil
I onion, peeled and finely chopped
salt, pepper and paprika

4 chicken quarters
I00g/4oz raw *serrano* ham, cubed
2 garlic cloves, skinned and finely chopped
I tomato, skinned and seeded

Heat the grill to high with the peppers on the rack. Grill them for 20 minutes, turning the peppers a quarter of the way over every 5 minutes. The skins will blacken. Place the hot peppers in a plastic bag and leave until they are cool enough to handle – 10 minutes – when the skins will come off easily. Peel off the skins on a plate, saving the juices. Split the peppers open and scoop out the seeds, discard these and the stalks.

Meanwhile heat the oil in a flameproof casserole and fry the onion slowly until soft. Rub salt, pepper and paprika into the chicken. Push the onion to the side of the pan and add the chicken pieces, frying them about 15 minutes on each side, until rosy and golden. About 5 minutes before they are ready, add the ham and garlic.

Chop the peppers on a plate, then mash with a fork. Chop the tomato flesh with it and add both to the spaces in the pan. Stir, cover, turn down the heat and cook for 10 minutes. Check the seasoning of the sauce and serve. New potatoes go well.

GAMBAS PIL-PIL

SIZZLING HOT PRAWNS
✪

SERVES FOUR

Everyone loves these, but you must adjust the amount of chilli according to your preference. A whole fresh chilli, dried chillies or a tiny amount of cayenne or paprika can be used.

8–12 tablespoons olive oil

350g/12oz raw prawns in the shell
1 fresh chilli, or 2 dried chillies, or ¼
    teaspoon cayenne, or 1 teaspoon
    paprika
2 garlic cloves, skinned and chopped
salt

Heat the oven to high for butane gas (220°C, 425°F, gas mark 7 at home). Pour 2 to 3 tablespoons oil each – Spaniards like more – into four individual ovenproof dishes (*cazuelitas*) and heat them in the oven. Meanwhile, peel the prawns. If you are using fresh chilli, remove the stalk and seeds, then slice into fine rings. Deseed dried chillies and crush into tiny pieces. Distribute the garlic in the oil and add the fresh or dried chilli. Divide the prawns between the dishes and sprinkle with salt (and cayenne or paprika if using), then stir in the oil. Return to the oven for 5 minutes until really hot. Serve with cocktail sticks for picking up the prawns and plenty of good bread for mopping up the juices.

Gambas pil-pil: *hot prawns flavoured with garlic and chilli*

POLLO AL AJILLO
A LA PARRILLA

BARBECUED OR GRILLED GARLIC CHICKEN
✪

SERVES FOUR
Spanish chickens taste as they are meant to, and this is an easy, but classic, way to eat them. Fish like besugo *(one for two), pretty pink* salmonetes *(one each), or about four* sardinas *per person can be cooked in the same way, adjusting times.*

1 chicken, cut into 4 serving pieces and
    backbone removed, or 8 thigh portions,
    or 4 legs
6 garlic cloves, skinned and finely
    chopped
2 teaspoons salt
1 teaspoon dried thyme (optional)
4 tablespoons olive oil
2 tablespoons lemon juice
thin strip of lemon zest, finely chopped
freshly ground black pepper

It is easier to cook chicken breasts if the two

end wing joints are removed, leaving only one. Remove excess skin and prick the thick parts of the flesh with a fork, then put the chicken in a shallow dish. Chop the garlic and then heap it up and cover with the salt. With flat side of a table knife, crush the garlic into the salt until you have a paste. Put it in a cup and add the thyme, oil, and lemon juice and lemon zest. Spoon this over the chicken, peppering it and turning the pieces several times. Leave aside.

Light the barbecue, then let the flames die down to cook. Or heat the grill to high. Cook the chicken, turning it several times for about 15 minutes on each side, dribbling or brushing with the marinade.

Note. A warning! Do not put the cooked chicken back into the unwashed marinade dish, to serve. There is always the risk of transferring salmonella from uncooked to cooked meat.

Heat the oven to high for butane gas (190°C, 375°F, gas mark 5 at home). Rub the meat with the garlic cloves and then with salt, paprika and pepper. Put the garlic cloves into an oven dish, into which the pork fits snugly. Pour in the oil, then turn the pork in this. Roast a tenderloin for 35 minutes and a loin for 1 hour 10 minutes, basting after 15 minutes.

Meanwhile, bring a large pan of salted water to the boil. Add the macaroni and cook for 8 to 10 minutes, making sure to follow the packet instructions. At the same time, put the sherry over the meat and baste again. When the meat is done, remove from the dish and discard the garlic. Drain the macaroni and add it to the meat dish. Season well and stir so the macaroni is well coated with meat juices. Carve the pork into slices and lay it on top.

Note. At home buy a four-chop joint, about 800g/1¾lb, and have it skinned, boned, rolled and tied.

SOLOMILLO DE CERDO CON MACARRONES

ROAST PORK WITH SHERRY AND MACARONI
⭐⭐

SERVES FOUR

This dish from the Cádiz region is so easy to cook and to shop for. A tenderloin of pork is economical, while a four-chop loin, boned and with rind removed, is more generous with the meat.

400g/14oz pork tenderloin or 600g/1¼lb boned join
3 garlic cloves, squashed
½ teaspoon salt
I teaspoon paprika
pepper
4 tablespoons oil
250g/8oz macaroni
125ml/4fl oz *amontillado* sherry

CHULETAS DE CERDO CON ALCAPARRAS Y PIMIENTO

PORK CHOPS WITH CAPERS AND PEPPERS
⭐

SERVES FOUR

More capers are produced in Spain than any other country. When pickled they have just the acidity to balance fried food, as in this colourful pepper and caper mixture. Try it, too, with fried fish.

2 tablespoons olive oil
1 small onion, peeled and chopped
1 green pepper, destalked, seeded and chopped
1 red pepper, destalked, seeded and chopped
1 garlic clove, skinned and finely chopped

4 pork chops
1 teaspoon paprika
salt and pepper
2 tablespoons pickled capers

Heat the oil in a frying pan large enough to take the chops and fry the onion gently for 10 minutes. Add the chopped peppers and garlic and fry, stirring occasionally, until the onions are soft – about another 10 minutes. Sprinkle the chops with paprika – standard practice in Spain – and the salt and pepper. Fry in the pan, pushing the vegetable mixture to the sides, or piling it on top of the chops, until these are well-cooked on both sides. Roughly chop the capers, stir into the peppers and heat through. Good with fried paprika potatoes.

A Rioja *reserva* would complement the dish. Or try a Valdepeñas red; the better ones are made with Cenibel – the best Rioja grape.

Pork with peas and sherry

CERDO CON GUISANTES Y CHAMPIÑONES EN JEREZ

PORK WITH PEAS AND MUSHROOMS IN
SHERRY SAUCE
✪✪

SERVES FOUR

An easy dish for spring or early summer. Boned pork loin is widely available and makes two neat slices each. Veal is good too, but more expensive; ask for filetitos, which are tiny escalopes. Fino in Spain also comes from Montilla, and so is not sherry, but is well liked for cooking.

3–4 tablespoons olive oil
2 tablespoons chopped onion
salt and pepper
600/1¼lb boneless pork loin, sliced into 8 escalopes
2 garlic cloves, skinned and chopped
250g/8oz button mushrooms, cleaned and sliced
2 tablespoons flour

175ml/6fl oz *fino* or dry sherry
1.5kg/3lb peas in the pod, shelled
about 175ml/6fl oz stock, made with a
  cube

Heat 3 tablespoons oil in a flameproof casserole and put in the onion. Cook slowly until soft, then push the onion to the sides of the pan. Salt and pepper the pork slices and fry these over a high heat until browned on both sides. Remove to a plate.

Add more oil, if needed, and the garlic and mushrooms. Cook more slowly, stirring occasionally until they soften. Sprinkle with the flour and stir this in. Add the *fino* and bring gently to the boil. Return the meat to the pan, disturbing it well, then add the peas. Pour in just enough stock to cover. Bring to the boil and simmer for 20 minutes, covered, until both meat and peas are done.

Note. This is really a dish to show off fresh peas. However, frozen peas can be used; cook for 10 minutes only. Use brown (chestnut) mushrooms if you can get them.

SORBETE DE LIMÓN

LEMON SORBET
✪✪

SERVES FOUR
When it is so hot that all you want to do is sit in the shade and eat ice-cream, this is the freshest and most delicious ice of all. In restaurants, it is served spooned back into the lemon shells.

3–4 lemons
200g/7oz sugar
500ml/18fl oz water
2 large egg whites

Take strips of zest from the lemons with a potato peeler and put them in a saucepan with the sugar and water. Bring to the boil, then boil for 5 minutes without stirring. Cool and strain. Squeeze the lemon juice and add.

Turn the lemon liquid into a freezerproof container and freeze for about 2 hours until slushy. Beat with a fork, then freeze again for about 30 minutes. Remove from the freezer and beat again. Whisk the egg whites until soft peaks form and fold into the ice. Freeze again for about 1 hour.

Note. At home – or if you are lucky enough to have an electric mixer on holiday – leave the ice until almost stiff. Then put it in the mixer and whisk it. Add the whisked egg whites in large dollops. This is whisked into the ice, which will go almost white. You can eat the sorbet immediately or refreeze it.

Lemon sorbet, light and cooling

SANGRÍA

CHILLED RED WINE AND
CITRUS FRUIT PUNCH
✪

SERVES FOUR

Some sangrías *contain brandy, but I think the nicest ones are those that are quite light. In the south, where this drink is most often made, the red wines are very high in alcohol – lethal when it's sunny! This* sangría *is quite sweet, the way the Spanish like it. If you use soda water instead of fizzy lemon, stir in a couple of tablespoons of caster sugar first.*

8–10 ice cubes
4 oranges
2 lemons
½ cinnamon stick or I teaspoon ground cinnamon
I litre bottle red wine, well chilled
750ml/1¼ pints fizzy lemonade, well chilled

Sangría – delicious red wine punch

Put the ice cubes into a jug that will hold at least 2 litres/3½ pints. Take a thin strip of zest from one orange and one lemon. Add these, with the cinnamon, to the jug. Squeeze and add all the juice, with the red wine. Chill in the refrigerator for a couple of hours. Top up with fizzy lemonade just before serving.

LIMONADA FRESCA

LEMONADE
✪

Small children can make this themselves. It is full of vitamin C and a fraction of the price of bought drinks. One particular brand of flower honey in Spain is sold with a snap-shut pourer, which is ideal for this. For one glass, squeeze the juice from 1 lemon and pour into a tall glass with 2 or 3 ice cubes. Add 1 tablespoon sugar or honey, then top up with cold water. Stir and drink.

Practical Information

Above: *street markets are a Spanish way of life*
Right: *vast numbers of places to eat make the choice bewildering*

SELF CATERING

Your Spanish kitchen is unlikely to contain a teapot, pepper mill or egg cups, and it is worth taking your favourite knife with you. The pans will be different shapes from those at home, so it may be easier to cook the Spanish way rather than trying to reproduce recipes from home without the proper equipment. Investigate your cooking facilities before you start shopping. The tops of Spanish stoves are often very small, limiting you to two pans. Ovens are small too – and the butane gas type, which is common, has no regulator, only high and low settings. Many Spaniards cook on the barbecue outside; this is both easy and fun. Instant coffee is very expensive in Spain, but supermarkets stock most normal commodities.

SAFE WATER

In public places drinking fountains are marked *agua potable* – don't drink from them otherwise. In some places tap water does not taste particularly nice and Spaniards drink bottled water at the table. If you suspect the water, avoid eating lettuce washed in it and make your ice cubes with mineral water.

MINOR ILLNESSES

For upset tummies, induced by eating and drinking, kaolin tablets solidify things. For infections from bugs in water or food, Lomotil is very effective. Too much sun can also make you feel ill and Spanish chemists (*farmacía*) stock the normal aspirins, etc.

TIGHT BUDGET

You will be agreeably surprised at the cost of food and drink in Spain – from the price of gin to the cost of eating out. In the humbler places, about £5 will buy you a three-course meal with wine. Bars everywhere supply hot food – and a *ración* is enough for a main course. Much the same dishes are offered in restaurants of different categories. It makes sense, therefore, not to eat in cafés with a view – even if you choose to drink there. They are always more expensive.

Carafe wine (the house choice) is always cheaper than bottles. Drink it with mineral water – though many Spaniards cheerfully use *La Casera* (fizzy lemonade). Water is now usually good and a jug of water with ice (*con hielo*) will cost nothing. At home, teach children to make drinks with real lemons (see recipe on page 116): cheaper and nicer than bought drinks. Every eating establishment is obliged by law to offer a three-course meal with bread and wine for a set price – often very good value.

Eat what others are eating, like the *plato del día* (dish of the day). Bean or vegetable dishes come as a course before the meat and can be very filling – enough for the meal in many cases, They can also be paired with soup or eggs, though these are all really alternatives. Adapt to local food, rather than looking for what you eat at home. TORTILLAS are very filling and come with lots of variations. Fresh grilled sardines are cheaper than other fish and very good. Avoid eating shellfish out – buy your prawns fresh in the market and cook them yourself. Recipes in restaurants are very simple anyway. Give up beef – it is not always good in Spain; pork is a better choice.

You can also take advantage of the large Spanish portions to share salads or a starter. Fruit is cheaper than dessert and normally two fruits are brought. Out shopping, street markets are weekly in most towns and villages, and there are bargains if you are on holiday for more than a week.

Finally, make the most of your holiday to eat luxuries that are expensive at home. In Spain you can afford to buy avocados by the kilo, and strawberries and artichokes in season cost little. Gorge on oranges at *5 pesetas* each, and wonderful tomatoes. These really are a bargain!

ESSENTIALS FOR TRAVELLERS

SPECIAL EVENTS

Spanish festivals are enormous fun but they disrupt shopping and banks, and restaurants may be closed just before them, and are booked up during them. The Spanish Tourist Office publishes a brochure every year, called the *Calendar of Celebrations*, with the dates of the main ones. However, almost every village celebrates its own saint's day.

The two public holidays that catch tourists unawares are Corpus Christi, the second Thursday after Whit Sunday, and Assumption, which is 15 August. If the latter falls on a Thursday, shops may be shut for four days. Since Saturday is a working day in Spain for many, a Tuesday or Friday holiday is usually added to the weekend. Also many shops shut in August for a month's holiday.

Little cakes are the universal festival foods, but sadly few are of any distinction. You will find exceptional roasts on festival menus, suckling pig and in particular baby lamb and kid at Easter, and pies called PANADES in Mallorca.

San José on 19 March is celebrated in Valencia with the Fallas processions, and in Madrid with BUÑUELOS, while Lent and Good Friday brings out a host of BALCALAO dishes. San Jorge (St George's day) falls on 23 April, and many places in Valencia and Alicante, and Alcoy, celebrate Spanish victory over the Moors with a simple rice and bean dish, MOROS Y CRISTIANOS.

Madrid celebrates its patron, San Isidore, around 15 May with BUÑUELOS and a fortnight-long festival. Corpus Christi, on the second Thursday after Whitsun, is marked by processions in Toledo and Sitges, near Barcelona.

San Juan on 22 June is celebrated with bonfires and feasting, particularly in Alicante, while Pamplona-Irunea toasts San Fermin on 6–14 July with bullrunning. Spain's National Day is 25 July, the Santiago Apóstal (St James), celebrated particularly in Valencia and, of course, in Santiago de Compostela, where TARTA DE SANTIAGO is eaten.

Asunción on 15 August means village festivals all over the south, with processions, flamenco and TORRÓN stalls. The biggest festival for San Matteo and America Day on 19 September is in Oviedo. This date is also the focus for the grape harvest festivals, which happen before picking in all the major wine-making places. In Logroño, trestle tables are set up in the streets. Here baby lamb chops are grilled over vine prunings (*sarmiento*) and served with lots of wine!

The 12 October Pilar festival in Zaragoza is one of Spain's biggest, celebrating the Virgin. It is also Columbus Day. Round the same time, in mid-October, saffron is harvested in New Castile, with a celebration choosing a saffron queen.

On 1 November, *Todos Los Santos*, the only shops open are pastry shops selling HUESOS DE SANTO, or PANELLETS in Catalunya. The weeks before Christmas see *turrón, figuritas de mazapán* and ROSCÓN DE REYES (yeast cake) on sale.

SHOPPING BASKET

The average price of items found in a typical family food basket.
- Loaf of bread 50–60ptas
- Wine 500–1000ptas
- Cornflakes 750 grams 300ptas
- Milk 1 litre 80–100ptas
- Apples 1 kilo 230ptas
- Cooked meat (ham) 250 grams 300ptas
- Cheese 500 grams 550–850ptas
- 6 eggs 75–100ptas

CUSTOMS

 YES From another EU country for personal use (guidelines):
800 cigarettes, 200 cigars, 1 kilogram of tobacco
10 litres of spirits (over 22%)
20 litres of aperitifs
90 litres of wine, of which 60 litres can be sparkling wine
110 litres of beer

From a non-EU country for your personal use, the allowances are:
200 cigarettes OR
50 cigars OR 250 grams of tobacco
1 litre of spirits (over 22%)
2 litres of intermediary products (e.g. sherry) and sparkling wine
2 litres of still wine
50 grams of perfume
0.25 litres of eau de toilette
The value limit for goods is 175 euros.

Travellers under 17 years of age are not entitled to the tobacco and alcohol allowances.

 NO Drugs, firearms, ammunition, offensive weapons, obscene material, unlicensed animals,

USEFUL WORDS AND PHRASES

PRONUNCIATION

○ Pronounce every letter, whatever its position in the word, eg leche (*lEh-che*). Exceptionally 'h' is always silent, as is 'u' in 'que' and 'qui'.

○ Accentuating the correct syllable is very important in Spanish. To help you, stressed vowels are in capitals in the imitated pronunciation, eg vino blanco (*bEE-no blAn-co*).

○ Spanish 'a' is pronounced like 'a' in 'father', but shorter; (and **not** as in 'hat' or 'hate') eg hasta mañana (*As-ta ma-nyA-na*).

○ Spanish 'e' is pronounced like 'e' in best or 'a' in 'Mary'; (and **not** as in 'he') eg bien (*byEn*), medio (*mEh-dyo*). 'er' is pronounced like Scottish 'er' in 'person', or like 'air' in English, eg supermercado (*soo-per-mer-kA-do*).

○ Spanish 'I' is pronounced like 'ee' in 'sheep', but shorter (and **not** as in 'right'). In the imitated pronunciation it is written as 'EE' if stressed, otherwise as 'I'. 'I' before another vowel is short 'guide', written as 'y' in the imitated pronunciation, eg si (*sEE*), pimienta (*pi-myEn-ta*).

○ Spanish 'o' is pronounced like 'o' in 'hot' (**not** as in 'low'), eg sopa (*sO-pa*).

○ Spanish 'u' is always pronounced as 'u' in pudding', eg fruta (*frOO-ta*).

○ Spanish 'r' is always strongly 'rolled', especially 'rr'. Children imitating an electric buzzer with the tip of their tongue come closer to the correct sound.

○ Spanish 'z' and 'c' before 'e' and 'I' are pronounced like 'th' in 'thing', eg cien (*thyEn*), zumo (*thOO-mo*). In some parts of Spain and Latin America this sound is pronounced like an 's'.

○ Spanish 'j' and 'g' before an 'e' or an 'I' resemble the 'ch' in Scottish 'loch'. In the imitated pronunciation it is shown as a capital H, eg naranja (*na-rAn-Ha*).

○ 'll' is pronouncd like 'lli' in 'million', in some parts of Spain and Latin America like 'y' in 'yes', eg paella (*pa-El-lya*).

○ 's' is always pronounced as in 'sing' (**not** as in 'rose').

○ Spanish 'v' is often heard as a 'b', 'd' as a 'th'.

HELPFUL PHRASES

○ **Could you say it again?** ¿Puede volver a repetir? *pwEh-de vol-vEr a re-pe-tEEr*
○ **I don't understand** No comprendo *no kom-prEn-do*
○ **Please speak more slowly** ¿Puede hablar más despacio? *pwEh-de a-blAr mAs des-pA-thyo*
○ **Please write it down** Por favor, escríbalo *por fa-vOr es-krEE-ba-lo*
○ **Do you speak English?** ¿Hábla inglés? *A-bla in-glEs*
○ **Where are you from?** ¿De dónde es usted? *deh dOhndeh Ehs oostEhdh?*
○ **Is there anyone who speaks...?** ¿Hay alguien que hable...? *ay Ahlgyehn keh Ahbleh...?*

QUESTIONS AND ANSWERS

○ **What...?** ¿Qué...? *kEh*
○ **Why...?** ¿Por qué...? *por kEh*
○ **Which (pl)...?** ¿Cuál (es)...? *kwAl es*
○ **How...?** ¿Cómo...? *KO-mo*
○ **How long...?** ¿Cuánto tiempo...? *kwAn-to tyEm-po*
○ **How much (how many)...?** ¿Cuánto (a, os, as)...? *kwAn-to (a, os, as)*
○ **When...?** ¿Cuándo *kwAhndoh*
○ **I don't know** No lo sé *noh loh sEh*

USEFUL WORDS AND PHRASES

NUMERALS

1	uno (una)	*OO-no, OO-na*
2	dos	*dOs*
3	tres	*trEhs*
4	cuatro	*kwA-tro*
5	cinco	*thEEn-ko*
6	seis	*sEh-is*
7	siete	*syEh-te*
8	ocho	*O-cho*
9	nueve	*nwEh-ve*
10	diez	*dyEth*
11	once	*On-the*
12	doce	*dO-the*
15	quince	*kEEn-the*
20	veinte	*vEh-in-te*
25	veinticinco	*veh-in-ti-thEEn-ko*
30	treinta	*trEh-in-ta*
40	cuarenta	*kwa-rEn-ta*
50	cincuenta	*thin-kwEnta*
60	sesenta	*se-sEn-ta*
70	setenta	*se-tEn-ta*
80	ochenta	*o-chEn-ta*
90	noventa	*no-vEn-ta*
100	cien (ciento)	*thyEn (thyEn-to)*
150	ciento cincuenta	*thyEn-to thin-kwEnta*
200	doscientos(as)	*dos-thyEn-tos(as)*
300	trescientos(as)	*tres-thyEn-tos(as)*
400	cuatrocientos(as)	*kwa-tro-thyEn-tos(as)*
500	quinientos(as)	*ki-nYen-tos(as)*
600	seiscientos(as)	*sEh-is-tbyEn-tos(as)*
700	setecientos(as)	*se-te-thyEn-tos(as)*
800	ochocientos(as)	*o-cho-thyEn-tos(as)*
900	novecientos(as)	*no-ve-thyEn-tos(as)*
1000	mil	*mEEl*

GREETINGS

- ✪ **Yes (no)** Sí (no) *sEE (nO)*
- ✪ **Please** Por favor *por fa-vOr*
- ✪ **Thank you (very much)** (Muchas) gracias *mOO-chas grA-thias*
- ✪ **Hello (goodbye)** Hola (adiós) *O-la, a-dyOs*
- ✪ **How are you?** Cómo está? *kO-mo es-tA*
- ✪ **Well, and you?** Muy bien *Y usted (tú)? mOOy byEn, EE oo-ste Eth, (too)*
- ✪ **My name is ...** Me llamo.. *me lyA-mo*
- ✪ **Delighted (to meet you)** Encantado(a) *en-kan-tA-do(a)*
- ✪ **This is my wife (husband)** Esta(e) es mi mujer (marido) *Es-ta(e) es mi moo-HEr (ma-rEE-do)*
- ✪ **Good morning** Buenos días *bwEh-nos dEE-as*
- ✪ **Good evening (goodnight)** Buenas tardes (noches) *bwEh-nas tAr-des (nO-ches)*
- ✪ **Tomorrow (in the morning)** Mañana (por la mañana) *ma-nyA-na (por la ma-nyA-na)*
- ✪ **See you later (till next time)** Hasta la vista (luego) *As-ta la vEE-sta (lwEh-go)*
- ✪ **Greetings** ¿Dónde está (están)...? *dOn-de es-tA (es-tAn)*
- ✪ **Have a good trip** Buen viaje *bwEhn byAhheh*

DIFFICULTIES

- ✪ **Go away! Come back!** !Vaya! !Vuelva! *vAh-ya, vwEl-va*
- ✪ **Excuse me (to get past)** Perdóneme *per-dO-ne-me*
- ✪ **I am sorry** Lo siento *lo syEn-to*
- ✪ **Can you help me?** ¿Puede. ayudarme? *pwEh-de a-yoo-dAr-rne*
- ✪ **Does it bother you (pl) if (I smoke)?** ¿Les molesta, si (fumo)? *les mo-lEs-ta see fOO-mo*
- ✪ **It does'nt matter** No importa *no im-pOr-ta*
- ✪ **Where are the toilets?** ¿Estén dónde los servicios? *dOn-de es-tAn los ser-vEE-thios*
- ✪ **Could I use your phone?** ¿Podria llamar por teléfono? *pohdrEEah lyahmAhr pohr tehlEhfohnoh?*
- ✪ **They are over there** Están allí *es-tAn ah-lyEE*
- ✪ **I (we) would like...** Quisiera (quisieramos)... *ki-syEh-ra, ki-sye-rA-mos*
- ✪ **What is this, that?** ¿Qué es esto(a), ese(a)? *kEh es Es-to(a), Eh-se(a)*

121

GOING SHOPPING

- **Is there a supermarket near here?** ¿Hay un supermercado por aquí *A-ee oon soo-per-mer-kA-do por a-Kee*
- **What day is the market?** ¿Qué días hay mercado? *ke dEE-as a-ee mer-kA-do*
- **I want (need) to buy...** Quiero comprar *kyEh-ro kom-prAr...*
- **I would like...** Quisiera... *ki-syEh-ra*
- **Do you have?** ¿Tiene...? *tyEh-ne*
- **Some (a little)...**Un poco de...*oon pO-ko de*
- **A couple of jars (cans)** Dos tarros (latas) *dos tAr-ros (lA-tas)*
- **A packet of...**Un paquete de...*oon pa-kEh-te de*
- **In oil (brine)** En aceite (salmuera) *en a-thEh-i-te (sahl-moo-Eh-ra)*
- **A slice (slab) of meat** Un pedazo de carne *oon pe-dA-tho de kAr-ne*

- **Bigger, smaller** Más grande, más pequeño *mas grAn-de, mas pe-kEh-nyo*
- **Can I help myself?** ¿Puedo servirme? *pwEh-do ser-vEEr-me*
- **Don't touch!** ¡No tocar! *no to-kAr*
- **Anything else?** ¿Algo más? *al-go mAs* That's it (no more) Nada más *NA-da mAs*
- **What does it cost?** ¿Cuánto es? *kwAn-to es*
- **This is the cheapest** Es el (la) más barato (a) *es el (la) mAs ba-rA-to (a)*
- **Go to the checkout (till)** Pase por caja *pA-se por kA-Ha*
- **Where are the drinks?** ¿Dónde están las bebidas? *dOn-de-es-tAn las be-bEE-das*
- **Do you have cold beers?** ¿Tiene cervezas frías? *tyEh-ne ther-vEh-thas frEE-as*

- **Where can I buy a can-opener (knife)?** ¿Dónde se puede comprar un abridor de latas (cuchillo)? *dOn-de se pwEh-de kom-prAr oon a-bri-dOr de lA-tas (koo-chEE-lye)*
- **Do you have cold meats?** ¿Tiene fiambres? *tyEh-ne fyAm-bres?*
- **I want to buy slices** Quisiera comprar tajadas. *ki-syEh-ra kom-prAr ta-HA-das*
- **I want fish for soup** Quiero pescados para sopa *kyEh-ro pes-kA-dos pa-ra sO-pa*
- **For baking** Para cocinar al horno *pa-ra ko-thi-nAr al Or-no*
- **Please clean them** Límpieles, por favor *lEEm-pyeh-les por fa-vOr*
- **Without heads and filleted** Sin cabezas, y en filetes sin *ka-bEh-thas, ee en fi-lEh-tes*

MEALS

- **We would like something to eat** Quisiéramos algo para comer *Ki-sye-rA-mos Al-go pa-ra ko-mEr*
- **Lunch** El almuerzo *el al-mwEr-tho*
- **Meal, usually lunch** La comida *la ko-mEe-da*
- **Aperitifs (and snacks in general)** Aperitivos *a-pe-ri-tEE-vos*
- **Bar snacks** Tapas *tA-pas*
- **Dinner, supper** La cena *la thEh-na*
- **Buffet or 'open table'** La mesa franca, buffet *la mEh-sa frAn-ka, boo-fEt*

TIME

- **When does the shop shut?** ¿Cuándo se cierra la tienda? *kwAn-do se thiEr-ra la tyEn-da*
- **Early, late** Temprano (tarde) *tem-prA-no (tAr-de)*
- **What time is it?** ¿Qué hora es? *kEh Ohrah Ehs?*

MONEY

- **I want to change some travellers' cheques** Quisiera cambiar los cheques de viajero *ki-sYEh-ra kam-byAr los chE-kes de vya-HE-ro*
- **Can I pay with this credit card?** ¿Se suede pager con esta tarjeta de crédito? *se pwEh-de pa-gAr kon Es-ta tar-HEh-ta de krE-di-to*

WEIGHTS AND MEASURES

- **Generous 2lb** Un kilo *oon kEE-lo*
- **1lb** Medio kilo *Meh-dyr kEE-lo*
- **½lb** Un cuarto kilo *oon kwAr-to kEE-lo*
- **¼lb** Cien gramos *tyEn grA-mos*
- **1¾ pint milk** Un litro de leche *oon lEE-tro de lEh-che*
- **17fl oz, generous ¾ pint** Quinientos mililitros *ki-nyEn-tos-mi-li-lEE-tros*
- **Half** Medio *mEh-dyo*
- **Twice that** Doble *dOh-ble*
- **A quarter** Un cuarto *oon kwAr-to*
- **A dozen** Una docena *oo-na do-thEh-na*

AT THE RESTAURANT

○ **What time do you serve meals?** ¿A qué hora se come? *a kEh O-ra se kO-rne*

○ **I want to reserve a table for four (six) people** Quiero reservar una mesa para cuatro (seis) personas. *kyEh-ro re-ser-vAr oo-na MEh-sa para kwA – tro (sEh-is) per-sO-nas*

○ **I prefer non-smoking** Prefiero no fumadores. *pre-fyEh-ro no foo-ma-dO-res*

○ **Is there a car park?** ¿Hay aparcamiento? *A-ee a-par-ka-myEn-to*

○ **The menu, please** La carta (lista), por favor. *la kAr-ta (lEEs-ta) por fa-vOr*

○ **How is it cooked?** ¿Cómo se hace? *kO-mo se A-the*

○ **What do you recommend?** ¿Qué me aconseja? *kEh me a-kon-sEh-Ha*

○ **Is it meat or fish?** ¿Es carne o pescado? *es kAr-ne o pes-kA-do*

○ **Does it include garlic?** ¿Lleva ajo? *lyEh-va A-Ho*

○ **May I change my order?** ¿Puedo cambiar la orden? *PwEh-do karn-byAr la Or-den*

○ **Can we have some more bread?** Más pan, por favor. *mAs pAn, por fa-vOr*

○ **We would like something to drink** Quisieramos algo a beber *ki-sye-rA-mos Al-go a-be-bEr*

○ **A bottle of red wine** Una botella de vino tinto *Oona bo-tEl-lya de bEE-no tEEn-to*

○ **Can you recommend a local wine?** ¿Puede usted récomendar un vino de la región? *pwEh-de oo-stEth re-ko-rnen-dAr oon bEE-no de la re-HyOn*

○ **We would like coffee** Quisieramos tomar café *ki-sye-rA-mos to-mAR ka fEh*

○ **May I have the bill, please?** La cuenta, por favor *la kwEn-ta por fa-vOr*

○ **Is service included?** ¿El servicio está incluido? *el ser-vEE-thyo es-tA in-kloo-EE-do*

○ **What is this charge?** ¿Qué es esta cantidad? *kEh es es-tA kan-ti-dAd*

○ **Do you accept this credit card (travelles' cheques)?** ¿Acepta usted esta tarjeta de crédito (cheques de viajero)? *a-tbEp-ta oo-stEth es-ta tar-HEh-ta de krEh-di-to (chEh-kes de vya-HEh-ro)*

○ **Thank you, this is for you** Gracias, esto(a) es para usted. *grA-thias, Esto(a) es pA-ra oo-stEth*

○ **We enjoyed it, thank you** Nos ha gustado, muchas gracias *nOs a goo-stA-do mOO-chas grA-thias*

SPECIAL REQUIREMENTS

○ **Do you have vegetarian dishes?** ¿Tiene platos vegetarianos? *tyEh-ne plA-tos ve-He-ta-ryA-nos*

○ **Is there any meat in it?** ¿Hay carne en este plato? *A-ee kAr-ne en Es-te plA-to*

○ **I'd prefer a salad** Prefiero una ensalada *pre-fyEh-ro OO-na en-sa-lA-da*

○ **I have to keep to a diet** Tengo régimen *tEn-go rEh-Hi-men*

○ **I cannot eat flour (milk, sugar)** No puedo comer harina (leche, azúcar) *no pwEh-do ko-mEr a-rEE-na, (lEh-che, a-thOO-kar)*

○ **I am diabetic** Soy diabético(a) *sOy dya-bEh-ti-ko*

○ **I am allergic to mussels, (shellfish)** Soy alérgico(a) a los mejillones (mariscos) *sOy a-lEr-Hi-ko a los me-Hil-]yO-nes (ma-rEE-kos)*

○ **I can't eat fried food** No puedo comer los platos fritos *no pweh-do ko-mer los fritos frEE-tos*

○ **I can't eat it, because I'm on a diet** No puedo comerlo porque tengo régimen *no pwEh-do ko-Eer-lo por-kEh tEn-go rEh-Hi-rnen*

○ **Is it very spicy (hot)?** ¿Es picante? *es pi-kAn-te -tas frEE-tas por fa-vOr*

○ **Can you bring some (a few) serviettes?** ¿Puede traernos (algunas) servil-letas? *pwEh-de tra-Er-nos (al-gOO-nas) ser-vil-lyEh-tas*

○ **Another plate, please** Otro Plato por favor *O-tro plA-to por fa-vOr*

○ **Some (two) spoons** Unas (dos) cucharas *OO-nas (dos) koo-chA-ras*

○ **Some teaspoons** Unas cucharillas *OO-nas koo-cha-rEEl-lyas*

○ **Have you got a high chair, please?** ¿Tiene una silla alta, por favor? *tyeh-ne OO-na sEEl-lya Al-ta por favor*

○ **Please could you warm up the baby's bottle?** ¿Puede calentar el biberón de bebé? *pwEh-de ka-lEn-tar el bi-be-rOn del be-bEh*

CONVERSION TABLES

NOTES ON USING THE RECIPES

Weights and measures are written in metric and imperial. Follow only one set of measure as they are not interchangeable.

ABBREVIATIONS

Metric	Imperial
g – gram or gramme	oz – ounce
kg – kilogram	lb – pound
ml – millilitre	fl oz – fluid oz

FLUID CONVERSIONS

125ml/4fl oz	500ml/18fl oz
150ml/¼ pint (5fl oz)	600ml/1 pint (20fl oz)
175ml/6fl oz	750ml/1¼ pints
200ml/7fl oz	1 litre/1¾ pints
300ml/½ pint (10fl oz)	2 litres/3½ pints

WEIGHT CONVERSIONS

50g/2oz	175g/7oz	700g/1½lb
75g/3oz	250g/9oz	1kg/2lb
100g/4oz	350g/12oz	1.5kg/3lb
150g/6oz	500g/1lb	2kg/4lb

SPOON MEASURES

Spoon measures refer to the standard measuring spoons and all quantities are level unless otherwise stated. Do not use table cutlery and serving spoons as their capacity varies.
½ teaspoon – 2.5ml
1 teaspoon – 5ml
1 tablespoon – 15ml (3 teaspoons)

OVEN TEMPERATURES

The following settings are used in the recipes in this book, providing centigrade, Fahrenheit and gas settings. However, cooking facilities in holiday accommodation may be limited or oven settings may be different or unreliable, therefore watch dishes carefully when baking in unfamiliar appliances.

110°C	225°F	gas ¼
120°C	250°F	gas ½
140°C	275°F	gas 1
150°C	300°F	gas 2
160°C	325°F	gas 3
180°C	350°F	gas 4
190°C	375°F	gas 5
200°C	400°F	gas 6
220°C	425°F	gas 7
230°C	450°F	gas 8
240°C	475°F	gas 9

AMERICAN MEASURES AND TERMS

Liquids:	Imperial	American
	5fl oz	⅔ cup
	8fl oz	1 cup
	10fl oz	1⅓ cups
	16fl oz	2 cups
	20fl oz (1 pint)	2½ cups

Solids: Whole pounds and fractions of a pound are used for some ingredients, such as butter, vegetables and meat. Cup measures are used for storecupboard foods, such as flour, sugar and rice. Butter is also measured by sticks.

	Imperial	American
Butter	8oz	1 cup (2 sticks)
Cheese, grated hard	4oz	1 cup
Flour	4oz	1 cup
Haricot beans, dried	6oz	1 cup
Mushrooms, sliced	8oz	2½ cups
Olives, whole	4oz	1 cup
Parmesan cheese, grated	1oz	3 tablespoons, 2oz/⅓ cup
Peas, shelled	4oz	1 cup
Raisins	6oz	1 cup
Rice (uncooked)	8oz	1 cup

Acknowledgements
The Automobile Association wishes to thanks the following photographers and libraries for their assistance in the preparation of this book.

ANTHONY BLAKE PHOTO LIBRARY F/C (d) (Rosenfeld), 43, 72, 85, 87, 88 (Gerrit Buntrock), 96 (J. Lee Studios); CEPHAS PICTURE LIBRARY 45 (Michael Barberousse); JAMES DAVIS TRAVEL PHOTOGRAPHY B/C, 28, 33, 68, 97b; EYE UBIQUITOUS 6, 48, 60, 78, 93; IMAGE BANK 15b, 75a, 80/1, 99; IMAGES COLOUR LIBRARY F/C (b).

All remaining pictures are held in the Association's own library (AA PHOTO LIBRARY): P BAKER 5b; M CHAPLOW 1, 2, 11b, 12/13, 35, 36, 38, 40, 52, 57, 62, 91a, 91b, 97a, 100, 101a, 104a, 105, 106a, 108, 109, 110a, 111, 112a, 113, 114a, 115a, 116a, 117b; S L DAY 101b; J EDMANSON F/C (c), 14b, 19, 23, 55, 66, 75b, 117a; P ENTICKNAP 16b, 17, 18b, 25, 76; E MEACHER 103, 104b, 106b, 107, 110b, 112b, 114b, 115b, 116b; A MOLYNEUX 47, 59; K PATERSON F/C (a), 5a, 7, 8, 9, 10a, 11a, 14a, 15a, 16a, 18a, 21; D ROBERTSON 10b, 82b, 94; J A TIMS 26; W VOYSEY 42; P WILSON 4, 30, 64, 77, 79a, 79b, 80, 81, 82a

Written by: Pepita Aris   Consultant: Bridget Jones   Managing Editor: Jackie Staddor